What you would like to know about
Karma

What you would like to know about
Karma

By
J. P. VASWANI

A Sterling Paperback

STERLING PAPERBACKS
An imprint of
Sterling Publishers (P) Ltd.
A-59 Okhla Industrial Area, Phase-II,
New Delhi-110020.
Tel: 26387070, 26386209; Fax: 91-11-26383788
E-mail: ghai@nde.vsnl.net.in
www.sterlingpublishers.com

What you would like to know about Karma
© 2004, J. P. Vaswani
ISBN 81 207 2774 6

Published by Sterling Publishers Pvt. Ltd., New Delhi-110 020.
Laserset by Vikas Compographics, New Delhi-110 020.
Printed at Sai Early Learners Pvt. Ltd., New Delhi.

CONTENTS

1. Is God Fair? 1
2. Why Me? 5
3. When Bad Things Happen to Good People ... 11
4. God is Fair! 13
5. The Law of *Karma* 19
6. The Choice is Ours 23
7. The Law of the Seed 25
8. The *Bania* and the *Sepoy* 29
9. A Subtle and Profound Law 34
10. Are We Really Free? 37
11. Do Unto Others ... 41
12. We Are Responsible for What Happens to Us 47
13. The School of Life 49
14. The Law of the Boomerang 52
15. The Good That You Do 53
16. Fate and Free Will 57
17. Are All Men Equal? 59
18. Change Your *Karma*! 61
19. More about *Karma* 63
20. Intimations of Immortality 65
21. *Karma* Is an Opportunity 68
22. How to Create Good *Karma* 69

23. We Create Our Own Destiny 71
24. The Two Selves Within You 74
25. Types of Karma 76
26. The Wheel of *Karma* 84
27. Freedom through Divine Grace 89
28. What is Fate? 95
29. Change Your Thoughts – Change Your Destiny 97
30. Practical Suggestions 99
31. Take Care of Your Thoughts 102
32. Say No to Negative Emotions 105
33. God is Watching You! 107
34. As You Sow ... 108
35. Take Care of Your *Sanga* 111
36. Accept! Accept! Accept! 114
37. Leave It to God! 118
38. Do Your Duty! 120
39. Be Like the Tiger, Not the Fox! 121
40. Attitude Counts! 123
41. *Yamas* and *Niyamas* 125
42. Be Vigilant! 128
43. Cultivate Consciousness! 129
44. You Are What You Think 131
45. Right Livelihood 133
46. Live in the Present 136
47. Do Good to Others 138
48. Help Your Brother! 140
49. Make Your Life Beautiful! 142
50. *Karma* – FAQs 144
51. *Karma* in the New Age 152
52. Thus Spoke the Great Ones 158

IS GOD FAIR?

As I move from place to place, meeting people, offering them the message of the *atman*, the message of hope, love and peace, time and again people have asked me this question: Is God fair? Our life on this earth is full of pleasant and unpleasant experiences. We pass through difficult times as well as enjoyable times. And even as we move along the pathways of life a period comes - a time comes in the life of each one of us, when we are confronted by the question: Is God fair?

There are times when we are happy; we laugh and sing; we are content with the way things are; everything seems to be going our way; we have all that we need, and many of the things we want. We say, God is gracious; God is great; God is generous! But a stage comes when we hit a rough patch; we pass through a trying phase; we encounter not just one or two, but a series of bitter experiences. Nothing seems to go right with us. We are confronted by problems and sufferings whichever way we turn. It is then that out of the very depths of our hearts comes this cry: Is God fair? Is He just?

Some years ago, I met a young girl, who was just 12 years old. She was one of seven children. They lived a happy and contented life with their parents. They had very little to complain about.

Their father, so this girl said to me, was a wonderful man, who lived a clean, healthy, happy life. He had no bad habits whatever. He was not given to smoking or drinking. He did not indulge in selfish pleasures - he liked to spend all the spare time he had with his family, for he loved them all dearly. He was also an honest and hardworking man. He would often work overtime - just so that he could earn a little more money for the sake of his family.

When he spent time with his children, he would often speak to them of God and His holy saints. He would relate to them stories from the *puranas* and the great epics. He inculcated good values in his children and encouraged them to grow up to be good human beings.

One night, he complained of pain in the chest. By the time the doctor could be summoned, he passed away.

This girl said to me with tears in her eyes, "My father repeatedly told us that whatever God does is good for us. In every little thing that happens to us, there is a meaning of His mercy. Never ever question the Will of God. Never ever ask why God is doing this to you."

She found that these wise words were of no avail to her now. Her father had been the only earning member of the family - and now, the seven children and their mother were bereft, lost without him. "Why did God snatch him away from us?" she sobbed. "How could He do this to us? Is God fair?"

There was a sister whom I met. She had been married to a kind and loving man. Soon after their marriage, they went on a honeymoon. They were away for a fortnight - which she found to be the most beautiful period of her life. Her husband loved her dearly, and took care of her with such loving kindness, that she was overwhelmed. He respected her least wish; there was nothing that she asked, which he did not give her. The honeymoon was indeed like a wonderful dream!

But all dreams come to an end - and as the happy couple were returning home, their car was involved in a terrible accident. A truck collided head-on with the vehicle, and the young husband was killed on the spot.

"It's true God gave me a wonderful husband," the woman told me. "But what's the point of snatching him away from me, barely two weeks after we were married? If he had to die so soon, why did God let me get married at all? Is God fair? Is God really fair?"

There lived a devoted couple who had been married for fifteen years. They longed for a baby, but they had been childless for fifteen long years. At last, God heard their prayers, and the wife was thrilled. She whispered in her husband's ears, "We're going to have a baby!"

They belonged to a wealthy family and they looked forward to the happy event with great anticipation. *Pujas* and special prayers were organized; hundreds of people were invited, and everyone was fed and received special gifts. They also gave extensively in charity – old age homes and orphanages were visited, and special service programmes were carried out.

When the baby was born, their joy knew no bounds. On the day of the child's naming ceremony, a grand banquet was arranged for friends and family. On the same day, the parents visited as many institutions as they could – they carried special gifts and food parcels and fruits for the handicapped, the underprivileged and the destitute. Truly, several lakhs were spent on the happy day!

But just a few days later, the wife passed away due to a mysterious illness. As the husband struggled to cope with this terrible loss, the doctors told him that his child was not normal. Barely a few months old, he suffered from a terrible syndrome – he screamed and howled like an animal; he flew into a rage and wept till he was blue in the face; he was uncontrollable. He was like a little wild animal.

The father was desolate with grief. "Why did God do this to us?" he asked himself repeatedly. "All these years, we got on well without a child. It is true we longed for a child – but we could have gone on without one, for we had each other, and we loved each other! Now God has taken my wife away – and left me alone to care for this child who is like an animal! What does He expect me to do? How does He think I can cope with it all? Is it fair?"

WHY ME?

Our rishis and sages have repeatedly emphasised one fact: every incident, every accident that happens to us, happens because we deserve it. Good and bad fortune are not handed to us on a platter; we have earned them through our own actions. Every action we perform, every incident that befalls us, is a reaction to our past actions. But when misfortune strikes, we fail to realise this.

There was a woman, who devoted the best years of her life to social service. She was pleasant and affable, obliging by nature and brought joy and comfort into the lives of those that were in need. She never ever thought of her own comfort and convenience, but went out of her way to serve as many as she could. Many were the people whose lives she touched, with her kindness and love.

One day, as she was walking along briskly, she suddenly lost her balance and slipped; but she picked herself up and carried on, heedless of the pain. A few days later, as she was returning home at night, she stumbled and fell across the threshold.

This time, she was worried, and went to her doctor for a check-up. The doctor examined her thoroughly and diagnosed her condition to be *multiple sclerosis*. She had never even heard of the term before. "What is multiple sclerosis?" she asked in perplexity.

The doctor explained to her that multiple sclerosis is a degenerative nerve disease which gathers momentum with the passage of time. It would affect her mobility in due course. She would not be able to walk without the help of someone. She could even be confined to a wheelchair. The doctor also added that the time may come when she could lose all bowel and bladder control. She would be dependent on others for all her routine chores.

The woman was dumbfounded. "Why me?" was her first reaction. "Why did this happen to me of all the people? When all my friends are living very healthy and very happy lives, why did this have to happen to me? Is God fair?"

A young man whom I knew well, was running a pharmaceutical business in Mumbai. He was intelligent and hardworking and the business flourished. But as he grew in prosperity, he became more and more inclined towards matters of spirituality. Entrusting his business to the care of a good friend, he began to devote more and more time to spiritual pursuits. His trust in his friend was absolute; he was confident that his business interests would be protected.

Alas, his hopes were belied by his friend's duplicity. Within a few years, all his assets were lost, and his business was brought to the brink of bankruptcy. He had to sell everything to settle the huge debts incurred.

Undaunted by this misadventure, he decided to seek his fortune abroad. He moved to Los Angles with the help of his friends, and here he set up a new business. He began to do well here too. He was especially proud of the fact that he was always honest and his dealings were all above board. As his finances began to improve, he began to dream of the day when he would be able to return home and resume the spiritual *sadhana* which he had been forced to give up earlier.

It was not to be. One day, two masked gunmen entered his shop. Holding their guns to his head, they looted the premises, taking away all his money and his goods. For the second time within a few years, financial ruin stared him in the face. On that occasion, he sent me the following letter:

As I write this letter to you, I shed bitter tears. Why is this happening to me? What have I done to deserve this misfortune? I begin the day with a prayer. I take the Lord's name each morning as I open my shop. I go to bed with His name on my lips. I have never, ever, harmed anyone in my life; I have never wished anyone ill. But I have been exploited and defrauded again and again!

Consider the fact that there were over a hundred shops in the arcade where my business is situated. All of them were untouched, while my shop alone was looted. Why did God allow this to happen to me? Is God fair? Is He really fair?

When they are faced with unpleasant or negative experiences, people react stereotypically: Why me? Why did it have to be like this? are the cries we hear at such times. The attitude of the sufferers is that they are victims - innocent victims - while someone else is the culprit, responsible for inflicting them with undeserved pain.

While we can sympathise with this attitude, we must realise that this will deprive us of the opportunity to reflect, introspect and thus recognise our own responsibility for our actions. In fact, by blaming others for our ills, we are only worsening the situation, or giving rise to new problems.

When we face whatever happens to us in a spirit of acceptance, we ward off very many negative feelings such as hatred, envy, malice and resentment. We rise above a sense of personal injustice and grow in the secure sense of Divine Universal Justice. In such a spirit and such a mood, despair and misery are kept out, and we are not overwhelmed by what happens to us.

A few years ago, I was told about this girl, who was a brilliant student at the University. She was doing her M.B.A. and she was expected to top her class. She was sure to get placed as a well-paid executive in one of the best companies in her city. Her mind was totally set on a professional career, and she was not interested in marriage at all.

However, her parents, being like so many parents we know, were very anxious to get her married. They had come across a handsome, wealthy young man who had flown in from the U.S. to visit his family. They were convinced that he would make an excellent husband to their brilliant daughter. They pleaded, coaxed and cajoled her into marriage with this young man.

They were married shortly, and the wedding reception was a grand affair. They went on a short honeymoon, and everything seemed perfect. Soon afterwards, the husband had to leave for the U.S. The girl had to wait for six months, until her visa formalities were completed. When everything was settled, she flew to the U.S. to join her husband.

He was not there at the Airport to receive her when she arrived. Just imagine the plight of a young girl who is flying into a foreign country for the first time in her life – there was no one to meet her. With the help of a kind-hearted fellow traveller, she managed to reach her husband's house. Her heart beating fast with fear, she knocked at the door. Sure enough, he opened the door. But it was not the happy ending to her story.

"Look here," he said to her harshly. "I don't want you here with me. I am married to an American girl, and you can't stay here with us."

The girl was thunderstruck. Nothing that she had gone through in life, had prepared her to face such a situation as this. She thought she had not heard him right. What could he mean – he was already married? Why did he have to spoil her life and ruin her career and her future? Why did this have to happen to her – she hadn't even wanted to get married in the first place!

You could not blame that girl if she raised the question: Is God fair?

A woman met me sometime ago. She had a woeful tale to relate. She and her husband had just one child – a son whom they loved dearly. He grew up to be a fine boy. He was intelligent, well-behaved and good-natured. He was endowed with many qualities of culture and character. He was studying to become an engineer, and was living in a hostel attached to the engineering college. One day, as he was riding on the pillion of his friend's two-wheeler, they were hit by a truck. His friend, who was driving the scooter, escaped with minor injuries; but this boy was killed on the spot.

When the news was communicated to the parents, they were stunned. The mother became unconscious, and had to be hospitalised. The father caught the next flight to the city where his son had lived, for he had to undertake the painful task of identifying his son's body and carrying out his last rites. While he was on board the plane, he had a massive heart attack. When the plane landed, the doctors who had been summoned to attend to him, pronounced him dead.

With tear-filled eyes, this woman said to me, "I lost my son, who was the apple of my eye. I lost my husband, who was everything to me. Now, I'm afraid I shall loose my sanity. Does God have no mercy on us? Does He have no sympathy for the souls whom He has created? Is there any justice in this Universe? Is God fair?"

I know a young woman who lives in Singapore. She is pious and God-fearing, and an active member of a Yoga Club in Singapore. A few years ago, she travelled to India along with her family members. They visited a number of sacred shrines. They met holy men, spiritual teachers whom they respected, and sought their blessings. Their trip to this country was veritably a pilgrimage. They returned to Singapore, spiritually rejuvenated.

A few days thereafter, their office premises were gutted by fire, and precious documents and equipment were destroyed. The girl was distraught. "Why did this have to happen to us?" she cried. "We visited India in a spirit of reverence, we sought the blessings of so many holy ones! How could God do this to us? Is God fair? Is He really fair?"

WHEN BAD THINGS HAPPEN TO GOOD PEOPLE ...

The story is the same wherever I go. People say to me: we have been honest and hardworking; we have not hurt or exploited anyone; we have done as much good as we could; and yet we have had to suffer. What could be the reason for this? Could it be that God is not really fair?

Some people believe that there are certain disciplines, certain practices which they must carry out – certain obligations they owe to God; and if they fail to fulfill them, they or their dear ones will be punished. One such woman met me when I visited Ottawa in Canada. She told me that she recited the second, twelfth and the eighteenth chapters of the *Gita* everyday, before she took her lunch. She also observed the *Satyanarayan* fast every month. But during a whole month, she missed out on the recitation and the fast, due to one reason or the other. The day after the missed *Satyanarayan* fast, her husband, who was perfectly healthy and normal, suffered a stroke, and has remained paralysed since then. The woman put to me the question that was uppermost in her mind: "Has this anything to do with my failure to read from the scriptures and observe the fast? Is there any cause-and-effect relationship between the two? Is God such a rigid taskmaster? Is He really fair?"

A learned Rabbi has written a book entitled *When Bad Things Happen To Good People*. In this book he tells us how suddenly, his three year old son was afflicted with a disease called progeria. Neither he nor his wife were even aware of a disease of that name. "What is progeria?" they asked the doctor, bewildered by the suddenness of it all.

The effect of the disease, the doctor explained, would be that the boy would not grow taller than three feet; that he would remain bald, and would age rapidly. Even as a child, he would have the appearance of an old man.

The Rabbi was grief stricken. "Why has God permitted an innocent child to become the victim of such a terrible disease?" he asked. "This little boy has never harmed or hurt anyone. Why is he being exposed to such physical and psychological torture?"

In his book, the Rabbi gives us several other cases similar to this one, and comes to a startling conclusion:

God is not omnipotent, all-powerful as we believe Him to be. God has limited power. Within these limitations, God can exercise his discretion. But there are certain grey areas where He is helpless. There are certain forces that He cannot control. And when these forces operate, God has no way of helping you. His power is limited and defined.

This is the conclusion that the learned Rabbi reaches in his book. "Here was I, who had dedicated my entire life to the service of God," the Rabbi tells us. "Why did such a terrible affliction strike my child?" Thus, he concludes, there are several incidents and accidents of life over which God has no control. When such troubles and trials confront man, God remains a passive spectator, who is powerless to intervene.

And so we return to the question which has haunted us again and again – Is God fair? Is God fair?

GOD IS FAIR!

If you look upon life as a journey, as many great writers have done, then you will know that this journey takes us at times through pleasant green meadows and lush river valleys; but at other times, this journey takes us through dry, arid deserts and dark, mysterious woods. Everyone of us knows this; everyone of us has experienced this in his or her own life. There are times when we feel on top of the world; there are times when we feel very depressed and despondent. When times are good, we are happy, we rejoice and offer gratitude to the Lord. But when things go wrong, we lose our equilibrium. We begin to question the justice of the Universe. It is at such moments that this question rises in the heart within – Is God Fair? Is God really Fair?

Before you try to answer this question yourself, before you finally decide whether God is fair or otherwise, I would wish to draw your attention to four very important points:

1. We have all been given the freedom of choice. God has bestowed on each and every individual, the right of freedom – the same degree of freedom that God has kept for himself. Man is free to choose – between vice and virtue, good and evil, selfishness and service. Man can choose to be selfish or unselfish. He can choose to be a sinner or a saint. He can choose to move on the path of evil, even become a criminal. He can choose to become a thief or a murderer. Equally, he can choose to move on the way of

virtue, he can become a God on earth. The choice is entirely his.

But remember, if the right to freedom of choice is vested within him, it follows that the responsibility for his actions also rests with him; for we cannot have rights without responsibilities. At every step on the road of life, we have the freedom to choose the direction in which we move.

Now, if I choose to move on the path of good, I go forward; I progress; I evolve spiritually. If I choose to move on the path of evil, I regress; I am pushed backwards. If I choose wrong over right, evil over good, how can I blame God for what results from my action?

This is the difference between men and animals. Animals do not have a mind or will of their own, to act as per their choice. They act without ulterior motive. They are only impelled by blind instincts. Suppose a man is crossing a jungle; he is confronted by a hungry man-eater who leaps on him, attacks him, tears his flesh to pieces and feeds on him! How can any blame accrue to the animal in this terrible incident? The animal was hungry; it killed and ate its victim. It was only acting according to its instincts, for it can act in no other way.

Now, if you or I were hungry, we *do* have a choice. We can lay our hand on the nearest chicken or lamb that we find, kill the dumb, defenceless animal, and feed on its flesh. Or we can shun this kind of violence, and choose the food of *ahimsa*, in the form of fruits and vegetables. The choice is ours, and the responsibility for our action rests with us. If we make the wrong choice, we must prepare to face up to its unpleasant consequences.

We have no right to take away the life of a creature, just to satisfy our appetites. Life, after all, is God's gift, and when I cannot bestow life on any creature, what right do I have to take it away? When we make the choice between good and evil, right and wrong, we determine the consequences of our own action. If we choose right, we attain happiness; if we choose wrong, we have to confront distress and misery. Amidst joy and pleasure and success, we invariably forget God; but the moment sorrow strikes, we rush to God with prayers and entreaties. We complain, "What have You done? Why is this happening to me?"

The *Upanishads* too, speak to us of the choice that we have before us. Here, it is referred to as *shreya* and *preya*. *Shreya* is the good; *preya* is the pleasant. It is the pleasant that attracts us; we are seekers of pleasure; we run after pleasure - and finally, we are so caught up in pleasure, that we are entrapped. But it is the choice we have made!

The path of *shreya*, the path of good, is a steep path; it is a rough and a rugged path; it is a stony and thorny path. In contrast, the path of *preya* is smooth and slippery, you can glide on the path without any resistance – but you slide to your doom! When you move on the path of *shreya*, you struggle, you suffer, but you are moving towards your higher destiny.

The choice is yours. Whatever the path you choose, you exercise your choice. Now, if I have chosen the path, and I have encountered a bitter experience which I cannot swallow, how can I question God's justice? Is it fair on my part to ask, "Is God fair?" Is it fair to blame God for the choices that I have made?

2. Life gives us many compensations and rewards – many more compensations and rewards than punishments and defeats. As I said earlier, life is a series of experiences. When we are passing through a difficult period, when we are confronted by experiences of misery and misfortune, adversity, illness, death, defeat and depression, we lament,

we complain of God's injustice, we begin to ask, "Why is this happening to me?"

But on the other hand, when we are passing through a happy phase, when we are blessed with special favours from God, it does not occur to any of us to tell God, "Why have you given me such happiness? I don't deserve it!"

There are numerous occasions in life when people get things that they never expected, or things that they have longed for all their life. After a long and frustrating wait, childless couples are blessed with offspring. Someone in dire need of money hits a jackpot. Another gets a long-awaited promotion. None of them ever think of telling God, "Why have you done this to me?" They simply assume that they have every right to the happiness that has come their way; they take it all for granted.

3. God's tender mercy to us is boundless – if only we took the trouble to realize the extent of His kindness. To people who come to me with bitter complaints against life, I pass on two sheets of paper. On one sheet I ask them to write all the cruel, the unfair, the unjust, the tyrannical, the dishonest and crooked things that they have done. On the other one, I ask them to write down all the good, the noble, the unselfish deeds that they have done in their lifetime. This is an exercise I recommend to you also, for it can be a real eye-opener for you.

When you have prepared these two lists, you will find that one list is much longer than the other. They do not balance each other. When you go through the lists, you will surely fold your hands in prayer before God and tell Him, "God, be merciful to me, please forgive me, for all the wrong deeds I have done!"

This is the case with most people - that their bad actions will by far outweigh the few good deeds they may have done. With such certain knowledge of our own balance-sheet of right and wrong, how can anyone of us claim that God has been unfair, unjust to us?

4. The last and the most important thing we must note is that whenever suffering comes to us, God always gives us the strength and wisdom to bear the suffering. For these are just two sides of the same coin – sorrow and wisdom; suffering and endurance. Look at the coin – on one side is suffering; on the other side is the wisdom and the strength to bear that suffering. Never, ever does God send suffering to us, unaccompanied by the strength and wisdom to cope with it. That is why we continue to live, that is how mankind has survived personal and public calamities, and still continues to survive and flourish. The very fact that we are all alive and breathing, is a testimony to this great truth – that we invariably conquer suffering with Godgiven strength and wisdom.

There was a great writer called William Barclay, who has written inspirational books. He was also a brilliant preacher. He loved his daughter dearly, for she was his only child. When he was making preparations to celebrate her wedding, the girl lost her life in a tragic drowning incident. Barclay said on that occasion, "I have no quarrel with Jesus. I am not concerned with whether or not he could have prevented the storm which caused my daughter's death. But I do know this for certain – He has quelled the inner storm that raged within my heart."

True it is, that with every suffering comes the healing mercy of God.

There was a man, who lost his only son in a war. He said to his friend, "When a man faces a loss such as this, there are only three ways out. The first is drink, the second is despair, the third is God. By God's grace, I have chosen the third option: Blessed Be His Name!"

With suffering comes wisdom and strength.

When you consider these points – the freedom of choice that we enjoy; the compensations and rewards that life offers to us; God's tender mercy to us; and the wisdom and the strength He sends to us along with suffering : is it fair to question God's justice? Is it *fair* to ask – Is God fair?

THE LAW OF *KARMA*

When Dr. Annie Besant, the founder of the famous Theosophical Society of India, was a young woman, she worked on the editorial staff of a prestigious magazine called *The New Review*. She was an intellectual woman, given to mature reflection and logical thinking. She gave birth to a baby who fell seriously ill soon after birth. The baby was running high fever, and as the temperature rose, the infant developed convulsions. Annie Besant was distraught at the sight of her little child going through these violent fits. She could not bear to think of her innocent baby being put through such suffering.

"They say God is all Mercy and Love," she said to herself. "Is this the kind of mercy and love He shows my child? What has this tender, innocent babe done to deserve such suffering?"

She virtually gave up all faith and belief in God after this happened. She became an agnostic. She spoke to preachers and religious teachers. No one could answer her questions satisfactorily "Where is God's love and compassion? Why is this child, who hasn't even hurt a fly, subject to such suffering?" They do not have an answer to such questions in Western philosophy, and Annie Besant got no answers.

One day, she came across a book by Mme. H.P.Blavatsky, entitled *The Secret Doctrine*. The editor had sent it to her for the purpose of review. As Annie Besant began to read the book, a new understanding dawned on her, and she was deeply impressed by its contents. One of the chapters in the book was entitled, "Karma and Reincarnation." She read it again and again – and began to see life in a new perspective. She seemed to have found, at last, answers to the questions she had been asking. Here was the only satisfactory explanation for her innocent child's suffering: it was nothing but the result of the *karma* of the child's previous births!

Enlightenment came to her as in a flash of lightning. She understood that the present life was *not* the first life, the only life lived by her, or her child. She had lived many, many, other lives before she had entered this body - likewise, her infant. It was due to the child's actions in those earlier births, that it was going through certain consequences in this birth. The infant had done something earlier, the effect of which, the fruit of which it was now faced with. The whole thing was crystal clear; the mystery was unravelled. She began to understand things, which were inexplicable earlier.

Because of this understanding, Annie Besant left her country, left behind her friends and family to come to India. She regarded India as the great land of the *rishis*, sages and saints who offered the most profound and satisfactory solution to life's problems. She came to live in Madras, and founded the famous Theosophical Society of India. There is a beautiful suburb of modern Chennai which is now named after her – Besant Nagar. India owes a deep debt of gratitude for all that Annie Besant has done, all the great services she rendered to this country. But she felt indebted to India for giving her a new insight into life and its meaning, through the doctrine of *karma* and re-incarnation. Once we understand this doctrine, the answer to the vexing question, "Is God Fair?" becomes very clear.

What is *karma*? The law of *karma* has been described
as the law of causation – the foundation on which this
Universe evolves. It is a Universal Law, an all-inclusive
Law which operates on the lives of all of us. It affects all
aspects of our existence – spiritual, psychic, physical; it
influences our thoughts, intentions, motives and actions. It
embraces our past, present and future, linked in a continuous
cause-effect relation. The impact of this law is inescapable
and inexorable. Its effect, reaction and response are
absolutely impartial. We could say that it is the law of
karma that upholds *dharma*, and maintains justice, equity,
order and balance in the universe. The law of *karma* operates
on individuals, as well as groups, communities, races and
nations.

Any action, thought or feeling generated by an individual,
brings with it certain indelible impressions, which are stored
in the mind as *samskaras*. Every act, thought or feeling
leaves behind a trace, which has the power to bring joy or
sorrow. These traces, or *karmic* residue, can bring about
consequences on three different levels:

1.   The type of next birth – bird, animal, plant or human
2.   Life span – long-lived or short-lived
3.   Life experiences – pleasurable or painful

Karmic actions lead to results that may affect us in this
birth, or in lives to come. Thus, *karma* is closely linked
with the concept of rebirth.

This leads us to the next question. What happens to us
in the interim between death and rebirth? Are all souls
condemned to be born again and again - caught in the cycle
of birth, death and rebirth?

According to *Vedanta* wisdom, there are four possibilities
open to the soul after death:

1.   For one who has attained enlightenment during this
life, there is total liberation from the cycle of birth and

death. Such a one attains *sadyah mukti* or instantaneous liberation and is not born again.

2. For one who has not attained liberation, but achieved purity of mind and devotion to Brahman, there is a force which pushes the soul beyond the pull of this world and towards liberation. This is *karma mukti* - gradual or sequential liberation. In this process, the soul is led along a path of light and so attains an increasing expansion in consciousness until liberation is attained.

3. For one who has tried to live a virtuous life, but is not ready for liberation, there is a finite period of existence on the astral plane, where the astral body experiences pleasurable conditions. This is known as *swarga*. It is not liberation, but a relative experience of pleasure. This finite period is brought to an end when the soul's good *karma* is exhausted, and the soul is re-born into a new life.

4. For one who has accumulated no good *karma* at all, there is the painful fourth alternative - a period of intense suffering. But this period also comes to a close when the sinful *karma* is exhausted, and the soul is re-born in a new embodiment.

Thus, in the first two cases, liberation is attained. In the third and the fourth, the soul must return to earth for the sake of its further evolution – after a period of either heavenly pleasure or hellish suffering. In these cases, *karma* will determine its next embodiment. For there are residues, remnants of *karma* that are not exhausted in the life-after-death state, be it heaven or hell. It is this residue or remnant that influences one's rebirth and life experiences. In other words none of us is born into this world with what is called a clean-slate. Even what we consider to be hereditary traits are in reality determined by the *karma* of previous lives.

THE CHOICE IS OURS

I must stress one important aspect here. While we all take birth with a *karmic* residue which determines our personality, we are also born with a certain freedom of choice with which we can succeed in accumulating new, good, positive *karma*. This choice, this freedom, this ability is available to every human being, and it is this which gives all of us the possibility of determining our own future destiny – not only for this life but in the lives to come.

To sum up: our life now is the product of the *karma* that we have accumulated in previous births; simultaneously, this present life is also the seed of the future of our soul. We carry our past *karmas* with us; and this burden may have to be borne by us even as we journey from life to life. The good and bad *karma* that we accumulate are entered in the credit and debit column of the account of our life. The balance is carried forward from one life into the next. This credit and debit is what we commonly refer to as *punya* and *paap*.

The law of *karma* is neither fatalistic nor punitive; nor is man a hapless, helpless victim in its bonds. God has blessed each one of us with reason, intellect and discrimination, as well as the sovereign free will. Even when our past *karma* inclines us towards evil, we can consciously tune our inclination towards detachment and ego-free action, thus lightening the *karmic* load.

A recognition and full awareness of the law of *karma* can help us to face life with a positive outlook; it can evoke in us the spirit of willing acceptance, and thus help us evolve as masters, rather than slaves of circumstances. Above all we can take control of our own actions and thereby shape our own future positively.

When we begin to understand the concept of *Karma* we will never ever blame God for anything that happens to us. We will realise that we are responsible for all that happens to us. As we sow, so shall we reap. Rich or poor, saint or sinner, miser or philanthropist, learned or illiterate – as you sow, so shall you reap. This is the Universal Law that applies to individuals, to whole communities, societies, nations and races. As we sow, so shall we reap.

THE LAW OF THE SEED

When you understand the concept of *karma*, you will realise why man has to accept both joy and sorrow. The *karma* of our previous births determines our destiny in this life.

The law of *karma* is the law of action and reaction. We have all heard of Newton's Third Law: Every action has an equal and opposite reaction.

Every action must lead to a reaction. The reaction may be immediate, or it may occur in due course. But no action can be cancelled. It will, inevitably, lead to a reaction.

The law of *karma* is also the law of effort and destiny; the effort of yesterday is the destiny of today. The effort of today will be the destiny of tomorrow. Every effort that I am putting forth today is going to be my destiny tomorrow – may be, in a future life. The efforts that I have put in during my earlier life, have become my destiny today.

The law of *karma* is also the law of cause and effect. Every effect must have a cause; every cause must produce an effect. Whatever is happening to us today, surely has a reason behind it. When our two hands come together, we produce a sound – a clap, as we call it. The sound is the effect; the cause is the coming together of our hands. The law of cause and effect is purely scientific and applies to all actions. What we have done in the past, has determined our present life; what we do today will determine our future.

Sadhu Vaswani referred to the law of *karma* as the law of the seed. He said to us, "Go and learn the law of the seed from any farmer, any peasant you meet. Any farmer will tell you that you will only reap what you sow. If you sow apples, you will reap apples. If you sow mangoes, you will reap mangoes. If you sow thorns, you will reap thorns."

Suppose a man sows thorns, and hopes to reap mangoes out of it – though he may hope and pray all his life, the thorns he has sown will never yield mangoes. The law of the seed, like the law of cause and effect, is universally applicable. We are all subject to this law. You cannot get a reprieve from the law of *karma*. You can save yourself, however, by improving your *karma*. The seed you sow today, shall grow into a tree and bear fruit; eat it you must, whether the fruit be bitter or sweet. We will have to face the consequences of our own actions. Nothing, no one, can save us from the law of *karma*. So powerful is the law that even Sri Rama could not save his father, King Dashratha, from the consequences of his *karma!*

When Dashratha was a young bachelor-prince, he went into the forest, on a hunting expedition. At that time, the young hermit Shravan Kumar was also passing through the forest. He carried his old, blind parents with him, in two baskets that were slung across his shoulders. The old people were thirsty; so he put them down in the shade of a tree and went to fetch water. As he was filling his pitcher with water at a pond, he was hit by an arrow and fatally wounded. It was Dashratha who had shot the arrow at him, for he had imagined that it was a deer which had come to drink water.

As Shravan Kumar lay in the agony of approaching death, Dashratha realized that it was a yogi whom he had wounded. He was horrified. He rushed to the side of the dying man; he shed tears of bitter repentance.

"Oh prince, I don't have long to live," gasped Shravan Kumar. "I request you to take this water to my aged, blind parents, for they both wait for me in thirst." So saying, the yogi passed away.

When Dashratha conveyed the sad news of their son's death to them, the helpless, blind parents could not contain their grief. In a fit of rage and sorrow, they cursed him. They said, "The day will come when what you have done to us will be done to you. Unable to sustain the loss of our son, we shall give up our lives today. May the fruit of your action rest on you! You too shall die of a broken heart, all alone! You too shall feel the loneliness of grief, as we do today. You will die because of separation from your dearly loved son!"

And so it came to pass, many years later. When this incident happened, Dashratha was a bachelor but he married three wives and begot four sons. Rama, his eldest son, was not only the apple of his father's eye, but the darling of the entire kingdom. When Dashratha decided to crown Rama as his *yuvraj* (heir to the throne), Kaikeyi, his second wife, took great offence. She wanted her son, Bharata, to be crowned *yuvraj* .

On an earlier occasion, Kaikeyi had saved her husband's life on the battlefield, and he had granted her two boons of her choice. Now on the eve of Sri Rama's coronation, Kaikeyi demanded her pound of flesh. When she asked for her two boons, King Dashratha readily consented; for he loved her dearly, and did not in the least suspect what was to come. Besides, his darling Rama was to be crowned the following day and this was surely an auspicious occasion to grant favours to his beloved queen!

Kaikeyi's two demands were spelt out: first, that Bharata should be made the king of Ayodhya, in Rama's place;

second, that Rama should be exiled to the forest, for fourteen years.

The kings of Raghukul were sworn to keep their word. King Dashratha now had to fulfill his promise to his wife. Rama was summoned, and his father's promise explained to him. Readily and willingly, he agreed to Kaikeyi's conditions. Even as he left Ayodhya, King Dashratha fell into a fatal swoon, smitten with the grief of parting from his beloved son.

Sri Rama was a divine being – an incarnation of Lord Vishnu. Even he could not free his beloved father, King Dashratha, from the bonds of *karma*. How then, can we ordinary mortals, expect to escape the burden of our own *karma*?

THE *BANIYA* AND THE *SEPOY*

A holy man, in his youth, had served in the army – that is, long before he renounced the world and took to the life of the spirit.

At that time, he had been posted in Rawalpindi. The British Government of the day had sent his platoon to Kabul to quell a Pathan uprising which was proving to be a threat to the local British authorities. One of the members of the contingent was an Indian sepoy, who met with a terrible fate. The mare that he was riding was a wild beast; getting out of control, it galloped away with its rider right into the camp of the Pathans. The fierce Pathan insurgents ruthlessly shot down both horse and rider.

The tragic news of the soldier's demise was conveyed to his family in India. His next-of-kin arrived to settle his accounts and take away all his belongings. The Army authorities paid up all the money and allowances that were due to him.

The dead soldier had entrusted a sum of two thousand rupees with the local *baniya* – the Army grocer. This was probably the custom among the sepoys at that time – whenever they were able to save some money, they would deposit it with the *baniya* for safe-keeping. The *baniya* decided that he would not mention this fact to the dead soldier's relatives. It was indeed, an evil temptation to defraud a dead man – the grocer yielded to it, and pocketed the money quietly. The dead man's relatives returned home, and the *baniya* was very pleased with himself.

Twenty years later, the holy man was brought face to face with the *baniya*, once again. Times had changed! India was now free. Pakistan and Afghanistan were independent nations. As I said, the holy man had left the army and acquired *sanyas*. Accompanied by a few of his disciples, he had gone to the holy city of Haridwar to take a dip in the sacred Ganga. On the return trip, they halted at a city called Saharanpur. It was here that they met the *baniya* from Rawalpindi.

"Don't you remember me, Swamiji?" he asked eagerly. "I am the same *baniya* who used to supply rations to your platoon in Rawalpindi. I have settled down here in this city after partition. I entreat you, Swamiji, to bless my home with your visit. You and your disciples must come and spend the night in my house. I cannot take no for an answer. Please do come, Swamiji, I beg of you!"

They could not turn down his persistent invitation, and so accompanied him to his house. He treated them with great courtesy and hospitality. An elaborate feast was prepared for them, and they were requested to partake of the food set before them.

As they sat down to eat, they heard the weeping and wailing of a woman from within the house.

"What's that?" enquired the holy man, startled. "It sounds like someone is in great anguish. Is any of your family members ill?"

"Never mind that, Swamiji," said the *baniya* hastily. "It is … It's nothing. I beg you to begin your dinner, for it is very late already."

The sobbing was so persistent that the guests were deeply disturbed. "Dinner can wait, my friend," the holy man said to the *baniya*. "Please attend to the lady – whoever she may be. She seems to be in great distress."

"I shall attend to her by and by, Swamiji," said the *baniya*. "But I beg you to partake of dinner and bless this home."

"My friend, we are not so heartless that we can eat in peace while some one in the house is evidently in pain and grief," the holy man said firmly. "Tell me who is crying, and why she is crying."

"What can I say *maharaj*," said the *baniya*, who was barely able to control his tears now. "My twenty year old son passed away just two days ago, and his young widow is weeping and mourning for him. She is barely seventeen years old. What can she do but cry?"

His guests were horrified to hear this. "It's not even two days since your son passed away!" they exclaimed. "What on earth possessed you to invite us home at such a time? How can you offer us a banquet when your family is in mourning?"

"I have done it with good reason," sighed the *baniya*. "If you want to know the truth, here it is." And he began to narrate his painful story.

"Twenty five years ago, when my contract with the army expired, I returned home. I set up a shop, and sometime later, I was married. Soon, we had a son. I brought him up well; nothing that he wanted was ever denied to him. When he was grown up, I found a beautiful bride for him, and they were happily married.

"All of a sudden, my son was struck by a strange illness. I spared no expenses to give him the best possible treatment. But the doctors could not cure him. I have lost count of the eminent physicians I consulted; but all their medicines were of no avail. He grew from bad to worse.

"One day, a friend told me of a *maulvi*, who was highly regarded by everyone. He suggested that I should bring the *maulvi* home for my son's treatment. I promptly brought him home, and he recited a few prayers and incantations for my son.

"When the recital was over, I realised that I had just two and a half rupees with me at home. I offered it to the *maulvi* and explained it was all I had at that time. I requested him to accept it with grace, and told him I would pay him later.

"As I pressed the money into the *maulvi's* hand, my son laughed out aloud! The *maulvi* was very happy. 'My prayers have had a very beneficial effect on the patient already,' he declared. 'I am confident that he will be up and about very soon.'

"When the *maulvi* had left, I went to my son's bedside and asked him why he had laughed. 'Are you feeling better now?'" I enquired anxiously.

"'Yes father, I am feeling much better,' he said. 'I am at peace now, for you have settled my account.'

"'What account, son?' I asked him, bewildered.

'Father, I want you to know the truth now,' he said. 'I am the Indian sepoy who was killed in Kabul, whose money you did not return to his family. I was reborn as your son, so that you could settle my old debt. The two and a half rupees you just paid to the *maulvi* has finally settled our old account. The purpose of this life of mine has now been fulfilled, and so I laughed out loud. Now, my time with you is over. I have received from you every *paisa* that was due to me, and I shall depart from this earth now.'

"'You cannot leave us!' I cried in despair. 'Why, you are just married, and your young bride lives in the hope that you will soon be better, and you two will lead a happy life together!'

" 'My new bride is none other than the wild mare which willfully carried me into the enemy camp, and brought about our death,' my son replied. 'It is to pay for this that she will now have to spend the rest of her life as a widow, mourning and lamenting my loss!'"

A SUBTLE AND PROFOUND LAW

My friends, some of you will find it difficult to believe this story. I do not know the background to these events - but I do know one thing. This story enshrines a great truth. *Everything that happens to us happens according to the law of karma.*

The law of *karma* is a great law, it is an inviolable law, it is a universal law. It is a law which is applicable to us all. Everything that is happening to us today is due to the law of *karma*. This we must never, ever forget. However, it is not easy to understand the working of this law. It is a profound law; it is a complex law. But it is, as I said, an inviolable law. It is a universal law of life.

It is our *karma* that is responsible for the joy and sorrow that fall to our share in this earthly life. But the first thing we must realise is this: our life, our personalities, our nature, our habits, our thoughts, our relationships with others, all of this is determined by the *karma* of our previous births. It is this that determines the pleasant and unpleasant experiences that befall us. Joy and sorrow come to us in turns because of our *karma*. We may be overwhelmed by a terrible catastrophe, or, we may hit upon an unexpected treasure. We may contract an incurable disease, or suffer due to ill health. All this is due to *karma*.

At this point, I wish to tell you about a seeker, a *jignasu* who wrote a letter to me, after listening to one of my talks on *karma*. His letter is so well-worded that I would like to quote parts of it here:

> You told us that the law of *karma* determines our life: as we sow, so shall we reap. You also stated that our action in previous births determines what happens to us in this birth. If this be so – what of those souls who are new-born in this world – those who have no previous births, and consequently bring no *karma* with them? Such people have sown nothing – what then, will they reap? What kind of *karma* will operate on them?
>
> We all know that India's population has virtually doubled in the last few decades, and there are now more than a hundred crore people in this country. Surely, all these people have not had previous births! It is said that human life is rare and precious, that it is a great gift from God, that one attains to this human life after countless other births in lower forms of existence. We are also told that all non-human forms of life such as birds and animals and plants are free from the laws of *karma*, for they are not conscious of their own actions. Therefore, I would like to ask you: On what basis of the law of *karma* do we weigh the actions of those who have taken human birth for the very first time? How does God judge them? Why are some of them poor and wretched, while others are rich and fortunate?

In answer to this question, I can only quote the following words from the Gita: *gahan karmo gati*. The law of *karma* is subtle and profound. We can never hope to master it, or even comprehend its truth with our mind or reason. To try to express its complexity in words, will be a mere exercise in futility, for this divine law transcends mere intellect. Just as we accept that there are certain deep scientific truths about this Universe that laymen cannot grasp, so also we must realise that in some aspects, the law of *karma* is too complex and too profound for us to grasp.

At a certain level, the law of *karma* seems so lucid, straightforward and quite scientific; and yet it is so subtle and complex that we cannot comprehend it by means of our intellect alone. While we can relate to it through comparisons such as I have used – action and reaction, sowing and reaping- it is far more difficult for us to apply it to ourselves, especially with regard to our own negative *karma*.

Let me illustrate this point with one of the issues raised in this letter – the question of the growing population. We must remind ourselves that our earth is not the centre of this Universe. Scientists tell us that there are countless galaxies, of which we know nothing as yet. We have no way of knowing what goes on in those unknown realms, or who lives there. How is it possible to know what forms of life exist beyond our small world? The great scientists of our age tell us that the planet earth is no more than a speck of dust in the vast unknown that is the cosmos. There are myriad planets and stars in which forms of life exist, and to transpose a life from one Universe to another is but child's play for the Maker. How then can we presume to talk knowledgeably about human birth and previous births? We cannot, *must not* dabble lightly on such issues. But the undeniable truth is that each and every one of us is bound by the bonds of *karma*; and our constant efforts must be focussed on liberation from these bonds. The question that we must face is this: how may we attain liberation from the bonds of *karma*?

ARE WE REALLY FREE?

Can anyone of us say with absolute certainly: "Nothing binds me. I am absolutely free"? Each and everyone of us is bound by the fetters of *karma*. Our ancient scriptures tell us of three different types of people: *nityamukta*, *mukta* and *badha*. The *nityamuktas* are those blessed souls who are not subject to the law of *karma*. Its effects can no longer touch them; for they have attained the Lotus Feet of the Lord; they are the ever-free, the eternally free, who are above and beyond the cycle of birth and re-birth, above and beyond *karma*.

The *muktas* are the liberated or emancipated souls; those who, through the grace of God or the grace of their Guru, have succeeded in liberating themselves from the bondage of *karma*.

The third type, *badhas,* are bound souls like us who are still bound by the toils of their own *karma*. Many of us, alas, are still in a state of ignorance about our own condition.

I recall a memorable evening, when my Beloved Master, Sadhu Vaswani, was pacing up and down the terrace of Krishta Kunj, his residence in Karachi. As he looked down at the street below, he exclaimed, "Prisoners! Prisoners!"

I looked down too – but I saw no prisoners. I saw the traffic, and I saw a number of people who were going about their business. But there was no sign of prisoners!

Actually, Krishta Kunj was situated quite close to the Karachi District Jail, and prisoners would pass by the house from time to time, as they were led out by their wardens for labour routines, or accompanied by policemen to appear in court. But on this occasion, there were no prisoners to be seen. Surprised, I said to him, "But Dada, I see no prisoners here!"

Sadhu Vaswani's reply still echoes in my ears. For long have I meditated on the profound wisdom of his words to me that evening: "Prisoners, prisoners of desire are the people," he said. "Alas, they know not of their bondage!"

Prisoners of desire are we all! We are bound by our own joys and sorrows. We are happy with what the world gives us; we take great joy in our pleasures and possessions. We celebrate the birth of a child, and we mourn over his loss when he passes away. We weep for a while, and then we beget more children. We are not aware of the fetters that bind us!

Those of us who become aware of our bonds, make the effort to seek liberation. This state of awareness is known as *mumukshatwa*, the desire to attain liberation. In this condition, our deep consciousness is awakened and urges us on the path of liberation.

Sri Ramakrishna Paramhansa was brilliant at illustrating the most profound and complex truths of life by means of beautiful and simple parables. One day he said to his disciples: "Everyday, fishermen cast their wide nets into the sea. A few fish are caught in the net. Many escape. Those that have escaped the net, swim about freely in the ocean; indeed, some fish are never ever caught. But those that are caught in the net, struggle to escape; and some of them actually succeed. They leap so valiantly, that they free themselves from the net, and get back into the vast and deep waters of the sea, where lies their true home. There are other fish caught in the net who also struggle to be free – but in vain. In vain they seek a way out, for someone to free them from the death-trap that ensnares them. They struggle persistently.

"But there are a few fish who are blissfully ignorant, happily unaware of their condition. They are content to rest passively in the net that ensnares them, unaware of the terrible and painful fate that awaits them."

In this significant parable, Sri Ramakrishna refers to the human condition; especially to the four kinds of people I referred to earlier - the *nityamukta*, those who are not touched by the bonds of *karma*; the *mukta*, those who, through their own efforts and the grace of God, liberate themselves from the bonds of *karma*; third, those who seek liberation and are struggling for it constantly; fourth, those who are so entrapped in their worldly life that they are unaware of their own bondage and seek nothing.

Gautama Buddha was one of those blessed souls who achieved liberation through his own efforts. Born the son of a king, he gave up his princely life and broke free from all worldly bonds that fettered him. He sought the way of liberation through enlightenment and succeeded in freeing himself totally from the bonds of *karma*.

Lord Buddha urged his followers not to waste their time and energy on futile speculations. "How did *karma* originate? Why are some people rich and others poor? Does God exist? If He exists, where exactly is He? These are unanswerable questions on which we have no need to dwell. Only realize the truth that you are bound by your *karma*. All your time and energy and effort must be focused on freeing yourself from the bonds!"

He narrated to his disciples the story of a man whose house had caught fire. The neighbours rushed out to help him. They tried to put out the flames and called out to him, "Come out of the house, or you will soon be reduced to ashes!"

The foolish man said to them, from within the house, "I will not leave this house until you answer three questions of mine: First, what caused the fire? Second, what is the exact temperature of the fire? Third, what are the chemical constituents of the fire? Until I get answers to these three questions, I shall not budge from here."

Incensed by his foolish stubbornness, the people cried, "You idiot! Is this the time or place to ask such questions? Get out of this burning inferno, save your skin. We can discuss these and other questions, after we have put the fire out."

But the man was adamant. "No way," he shouted. "I shan't leave this house until my questions have been answered."

Such is the folly of many of us today. We live amidst burning flames that threaten to engulf us. We need to make every effort to save ourselves, to quench the leaping flames.

"Man is burning," the Buddha repeated emphatically. "Some are trapped in the fire of hatred; others in the flames of envy, passion, greed or jealousy, ego and pride. Quench the flames! Quench the flames!"

Therefore, let us not waste our efforts in trying to figure out complicated issues such as population growth and the fate of new souls. The question that should concern us is: what should we do, what *can* we do to liberate ourselves from the bonds of *karma*?

The seeker who wrote to me, continued with his queries:

What is the nature of God's justice? Are we allowed to explain our motives? Does He give us the chance to justify ourselves? If perchance, there is a miscarriage of justice in God's dispensation, what does He do to set it right? And if such injustice is not set right, should we not regard God as unfair and unjust?

DO UNTO OTHERS ...

There is a story told to us from ancient Buddhist records. A wealthy jeweller was once travelling to Varanasi, on an important business venture. He had his own comfortable carriage drawn by horses, and a slave travelled with him to attend to his every need. He was looking forward to doing some lucrative banking business in Varanasi. He was sure he would be making a lot of money out of the new venture.

It was a pleasant day and the horses sped along the way. All of a sudden, the jeweller, whose name was Pandu, spotted a Buddhist monk, a *samana* walking along the road. Impressed by the saintly aura of the *samana*, the jeweller thought to himself: "This man seems to be truly holy and venerable. They say that the acquaintance of such a good man brings luck. I shall invite him to ride in my carriage to Varanasi."

The *samana* who was feeling quite exhausted by his long walk, gratefully accepted the wealthy man's invitation. "I am too poor to repay you with gifts," he said with humility. "But I shall be happy to share with you some of the spiritual treasures I have gathered from the teachings of the Enlightened One."

They travelled on together, Pandu listening with great pleasure to the inspiring discourse of the *samana*. However, their rapid progress was halted abruptly; for a farmer's cart laden with rice had come to a halt, blocking the road altogether. The lynchpin of the wheel had come off, and the farmer was desperately trying to mend the damage.

Annoyed by the delay, the jeweller ordered his slave to push the cart aside. The slave, whose name was Mahaduta, was a huge and strong man who enjoyed bullying weaker men and inflicting pain on them. He got down from the carriage and, without further ado, began to push the cart aside violently, upsetting its load of rice.

"You can't do this to me!" remonstrated the poor farmer. "I have to sell that rice in Varanasi by this evening. The money I make will feed my family for a month!"

The jeweller paid no attention to the farmer's protest. He ordered Mahaduta to overturn the cart and make way for his carriage. Before the *samana* could interfere, the slave had overturned the cart, spilling all the rice on the wayside. The farmer began to scold and curse – but when the big, burly slave raised his fist, he became subdued, although he continued to curse under his breath.

Appalled by the plight of the farmer, the *samana* jumped out of the carriage, and said to Pandu: "I must leave your carriage now. I am truly grateful to you for the ride, but now, I must assist this farmer, for he is the incarnation of one of your ancestors. The best way I can repay your kindness would be to assist him in his trouble."

"This wretched farmer is my ancestor?" said Pandu, incredulous with amazement. "That cannot be!"

"You are not aware of the strings of *karma* which bind you with this farmer," replied the monk. "Very many wealthy men are like you, spiritually blind. You do not know that you are harming your own interest. I must try to protect you."

The merchant was alarmed, and decided to drive on quickly, for fear that he would offend the holy man.

The monk turned to the poor farmer who was cursing loudly now. Quickly and efficiently, he helped him to repair the cart and reload the rice that had been thrown out. In a very short while, the work was completed, and the farmer's cart was back on the track.

"O holy man, I cannot thank you enough for your kindness," exclaimed the farmer. "Truly, the *devas* seem to assist you, for you have helped me to get my cart back on the road. But tell me, why should I suffer injustice at the hands of that horrible man, whom I have never harmed in any way?"

The monk smiled and said, "My friend, the injustice you receive in the present state of existence is nothing but the return of the same treatment that you gave to the jeweller in a former life. You are only reaping what you have sown earlier. Your present life is nothing but the result of the *karma* of your past lives."

"That is as may be," said the farmer. "But what did I have to do with that arrogant jeweller?"

"Why my friend," said the monk, "you are very similar to him in character, though you may not know it. Tell me, if you had been in his place, would you or would you not have behaved in the same way?"

Sheepishly, the farmer acknowledged that if he had been rich and powerful, he would have treated weaker men in the same fashion. But now that he had heard of the retribution that bad *karma* can bring, he resolved silently that in the future, he would be more considerate with his fellow human beings.

The rice was loaded and secured and, together, they pursued their journey to Varanasi. A little distance down the road, they came across a fat purse lying on the road. The monk recognized it – it belonged to Pandu, the jeweller. He picked up the purse and found that it was stuffed with gold. Whatever business Pandu wanted to transact in Varanasi, would be impossible without this purse.

The monk said to the farmer, "Here is a chance for you to teach the jeweller a lesson. It will rebound to your well-being both in this and in your future lives. The sweetest revenge is to return good will for hatred. I shall point out to you the inn at which Pandu plans to stay, and you can return the money to him. He will be ashamed and beg your pardon. You must tell him that you have forgiven him and wish him success in all his undertakings. For let me warn you, the more successful he is, the better will you prosper. Your fate depends in many respects upon his fate.

"If the jeweller demands any explanation for your behaviour, direct him to the *Vihara* where I shall be staying. Tell him I will be happy to offer him any explanation he seeks."

The farmer agreed to do exactly as he was bidden. They reached Varanasi by evening but bad news awaited the farmer. The entire rice market in Varanasi had been 'cornered' by a rich speculator, ie, he had bought all the rice in the market, thus closing the market down altogether. There was no rice left to sell, and the rice merchants had left town.

In the meanwhile, the jeweller had gone to meet his friend, Mallika the banker. The banker was in dire distress: he had undertaken a contract to supply a cart load of the best rice for the king's table that night. Now, the entire rice market had been cornered, and he could not honour his contract. This would ruin his reputation altogether.

They walked up to the inn, the banker lamenting his misfortune, and the jeweller wondering about the prospects of his venture. Suddenly, he looked for his purse and found it missing.

"I am ruined!" he cried in shock and anger. He ordered his carriage to be searched, but the purse was not there. Suspecting his slave to be the culprit, he sent for the police, accused his slave and had him arrested, bound and tortured cruelly, so that a confession could be extracted from him.

The huge slave was whipped and lashed till he was in agony. "I am innocent," he screamed in pain. "Oh let me go, for I am dying of pain. I am innocent, and I suffer now the pain that I inflicted on others. I am sure this torture is a punishment for my ill-treatment of others."

While the slave was being lashed, the farmer drove his rice-ladden cart into the inn yard. Finding Pandu there, he promptly handed over his purse. Mahaduta, the slave, was immediately released from custody, but disillusioned with his master, he decided to run away into the forest and become a dacoit.

In the meanwhile, the banker's eyes fell on the rice-ladden cart. Instantly, he beseeched the farmer to sell the whole lot to him, for delivery to the royal table. In sheer relief and gratitude, he paid the farmer triple the price that the rice would have fetched in the market.

Pandu received his purse, speechless with surprise. How was it that a man whom he had ill-treated just a few hours earlier, could do such a good turn for him? The farmer directed him to the *vihara* to receive further explanation from the *samana*, the benefactor of them both.

Pandu rushed to the *vihara* and fell at the feet of the monk.

The monk said to him, "I might give you an explanation, but I doubt if you will understand it, for you have shown yourself to be incapable of grasping spiritual truths. However,

I can offer you advice: treat every man whom you meet as your own self; serve him as you would demand to be served yourself: for our *karma* travels apace. Sooner or later it will come home to us."

"Please help me understand this truth better," cried Pandu. "I shall follow your advice, if you help me to unravel the mystery of *karma*."

"Here then is the key to the mystery," said the *samana*. "Even if you can't grasp it, have faith in my words. *Self is an illusion*. You must learn to see your reflection in the souls of others. Therefore, bear this in mind:

Who injureth others
Himself hurteth sore;
Who others assisteth
Himself helpeth more.
Let the illusion of self
From your mind disappear,
And you'll find the way sure;
The path will be clear.

WE ARE RESPONSIBLE FOR WHAT HAPPENS TO US

All around us in the world today, we witness violence, crime and needless bloodshed. People are often depressed and saddened by the human condition. All this is due to *avidya*, our ignorance. The vital need for us today is that our true consciousness may be awakened and that we may understand the great truth of the law of *karma* – that what we do unto others will inevitably, in the near or remote future, return to us in one form or another. This is an inviolable, inescapable law of life. If we perpetrate evil, violence or cruelty, these will invariably find their way back to us.

The striking illustration of this law is the story of King Dritarashtra in the Mahabharata. At the end of the Kurukshetra war, Sri Krishna comes to meet the Pandavas, who are now responsible for their aged, blind uncle, King Dritarashtra, for all his hundred sons, the Kauravas, have perished in the war. "It is time that I returned to Dwaraka now," Sri Krishna tells the sad, depleted family. "Tell me if there is anything I can do for any of you before I leave."

The blind, ageing monarch tells him, "Dear Lord! I have done no harm to anyone in my life. I have tried my best to be fair to everyone. Why, oh, why is it that I have been cursed with such a miserable fate? Not only has God deprived me of eyesight, but I have also lost the comfort of

the support of my sons in old age. Each and every one of
my hundred brave sons has perished on the battlefield! Why
has God been so cruel to me?"

"O King," Sri Krishna says to him, "Look deep within
yourself. Enter into your deepest consciousness, where you
will find the answer to your own question."

Dritarashtra does as he is told. He enters into deep
meditation, thereby gaining access to the astral self, wherein
lie rooted, the hidden memories of his previous births. He
realises that several lives earlier, during one of his many
human births, he had been a cruel and proud king. As he
goes out riding with his courtiers, he sees a magnificent
swan surrounded by its offspring – a hundred, beautiful
signets. In a ruthless and wanton act of cruelty, the tyrant
king orders his soldiers to blind the swan and kill all its
hundred offsprings ...

King Dritarashtra's question is answered. It is now clear
to him that his blindness and the death of his hundred brave
sons during this life, is solely due to what he had done once
in the remote past.

There was a time in this ancient land of ours, when
everyone was fully aware of this great and inscrutable law.
Being so aware, people considered the consequences of their
actions, and acted with caution and discrimination. Today,
alas, we live in oblivion of this Universal Law! If only we
would remember this great truth and act according to its
precepts, we would surely evolve into a new and noble nation,
worthy of our great tradition.

THE SCHOOL OF LIFE

To return to the question we raised earlier: Is God unfair and unjust?

There is no question of any injustice in God's dispensation. I say again and again: God is too loving to punish, too wise to make a mistake. His dispensation of justice is simple and straightforward. He has no policeman to catch wrong doers; no courts to conduct endless trials; no judges to pronounce harsh sentences on those who are found guilty. God's dispensation is simple. Each one of us has been given a field of life. We are free to sow whatever we want in this field, which is our *karma-kshetra*. Only one condition binds us; we must reap what we sow. We must eat the fruits of our own harvest.

We are sowing seeds every day, every hour, every moment in the field of life. Every thought I think, every word I utter, every deed I perform, every emotion, every feeling, every wish that awakens within me – these are all seeds that I am sowing in the field of my life. In course of time, these seeds will germinate and bear fruit. Bitter or sweet they may be – but I shall have to eat those fruits. No one else can eat them for me. Where then is the question of God being unfair or unjust to me?

The trouble is that man in his ignorance, commits errors and misdeeds. His wrong acts add up to his *karma*. His *karma* binds him to its consequences. What we must seek, therefore, is liberation from the bonds of *karma*.

Life is, in many ways, like a school for human souls. We have all come to this school to learn valuable lessons, to reach certain conclusions, to attain certain goals, that we may obtain knowledge of the truth that is worth knowing. We are not the bodies we wear; in reality our true self is the soul which is eternal and undying. The Gita tells us that the body is merely a garment worn by the soul during its earthly existence. The body is born and it dies. The soul is deathless, eternal; fires cannot burn it, weapons cannot cleave it; air cannot dry it; waters cannot drown it. This soul dwells in the body during our earthly life. We are born and reborn upon this earth, so that we may grow in perfection and ultimately achieve liberation – our true state.

We have come across naughty children, who complain to their parents that the teacher has been unkind, unfair to them and punished them unnecessarily. What the children regard as 'unfair' punishment, the teacher uses as an instrument of learning, a corrective measure which will set them on the right track. If the teacher did not adopt such measures to improve the child's behaviour, it is likely that the child may grow up to be a flawed human being.

It is in such a spirit that we must go through the trials and tribulations that life brings to us – such as problems, illness and sorrows. We are all students in the school of life; experience is our teacher, and it offers us valuable lessons that we may evolve spiritually, and attain the liberation that we seek. We will do well to remember that we have not come to the school of life to enjoy ourselves or merely indulge in fun and frolic. We have been given this life, that we may evolve, that we may raise ourselves to the heights of liberation. We pass through varied and very different experiences here; for the lessons that *I* have to learn are vastly different from the lessons *you* will have to learn. The law of *karma* is not punitive; it does not wreak vengeance, and it is the fine art by which we may eventually transcend the cycle of birth and death.

God is the very spirit of Love. His Law of *karma* works to put us on the path to perfection. When we love someone deeply, we want him or her to evolve into a good human being, to grow in perfection and appreciate the true and lasting values of life. God loves us deeply, and therefore, through the operation of the law of *karma*, he places us in such an environment where we may realise our *atmashakti* (spiritual strength) and awaken to the true knowledge of the Self. In our ignorance and immaturity, we may regard this as a form of punishment; but like the kind and caring teacher, God knows that these experiences are vital to our spiritual growth.

THE LAW OF THE BOOMERANG

We have tried to understand that everything that happens to man is of his own doing. In other words, man is the builder of his own destiny. Destiny is not something that has been imposed on him from without. He is the builder of his own destiny. He is the creator of his own fate; he is the architect of his own future. God has given man complete freedom of choice. Everyone of us, every human being has been given this freedom of choice. We can choose between good and evil; we can choose between *shreya* and *preya*.

My Beloved Master, Sadhu Vaswani, described the principle of *karma* as the principle of a boomerang. What you send, comes back to you! Do you gossip about another? You will be gossiped about! Do you send out thoughts of hatred and enmity to another? Hatred and enmity will come back to you, turning your life into a veritable hell!

Do you send out loving thoughts to others? Do you pray for struggling souls? Do you serve those who are in need? Are you kind to passers-by, the pilgrims on the way who seek your hospitality? Then remember, sure as the sun rises in the East, all these things will return to you, making your life beautiful and bright as a rose garden in the season of spring!

The law of *karma* is thus the law of the boomerang. It is an inviolable law that governs the Universe from end to end.

THE GOOD THAT YOU DO

The subtle effect of an action (*karma*) is to reflect the action back to you. The law of *karma* states that you are repaid by the same pleasure or pain that you bestow on others through your action. Here is a story that illustrates this point.

There was a woman who always baked an extra chappati, when she prepared the meals for her family. She kept the extra chappati on the window-sill for whoever would take it away. Everyday, a hunch-back came and took away the chappati. Instead of expressing gratitude, he muttered the following words before he went his way:

The evil you do remains with you:

The good you do comes back to you

This went on, day after day. Everyday, the hunchback came, lifted the chappati, and uttered the words:

The evil you do remains with you:

The good you do comes back to you!

The woman felt irritated. "Not a word of gratitude," she said to herself. "But everyday this hunch-back utters this jingle! What does he mean?"

One day, exasperated, she decided to do away with him. "I shall get rid of this hunch-back," she said to herself. And what did she do? She added poison to the chappati she prepared for him! As she was about to keep it on the window-sill, her hands trembled. "What is this that I am doing?" she said to herself. Immediately, she threw the chappati into the fire and prepared another one and kept it on the window-sill. Sure enough, the hunch-back came, picked up the chappati and muttered the words:

The evil you do remains with you:
The good you do comes back to you!

The hunch-back proceeded on his way, blissfully unaware of the war raging in the mind of the woman.

Everyday, as the woman placed the chappati on the window-sill she offered a prayer for her son who had gone abroad to seek his fortune. For many months she had had no news of him. She prayed for the safe return of her son.

That evening, there was a knock on the door. As she opened it she was surprised to find her son standing in the doorway. He had grown thin and lean. His garments were tattered and torn. He was hungry, starved and weak. Looking at his mother, he said: "Mother, it's a miracle that I have been able to reach you. When I was but a mile away, I was so famished that I collapsed. Just then, an old hunchback passed by. I begged of him for a morsel of food, and he was kind enough to give me a whole chappati. As he gave it to me, he said, 'This is what I eat everyday. Today, I shall give it to you, for your need is greater than mine!'"

As the mother heard those words she turned pale. She leaned against the door for support. She remembered the poisoned chappati she had made that morning. Had she not hearkened to the voice of her conscience and burnt it in the fire, that chappati would have cost her, her son's life. It was then that she realised the meaning of the hunch-back's words:

The evil you do remains with you:
The good you do comes back to you!

I read an incident sometime ago concerning a Polish Air Force pilot, Roman Tursky. He was flying his plane over Germany when he made a forced landing on German soil.

He sent his plane for repairs and spent the night in a hotel. The next morning, as he left his room, and was walking in the corridor, a little man came running and collided against him. Roman Tursky naturally felt offended. But as he looked at the face of the little man, he found it pale with fright.

The man cried, "Gestapo! Gestapo!"

Gestapo is the German Secret Police. It was obvious that the man was being hounded by the Secret Police and he wanted to escape. Roman Tursky understood the situation and instantly pushed the man into his room, under his bed. Soon thereafter the police came in and interrogated Tursky. He did not understand their language, and the police went away.

The pilot offered to take this man to Warsaw where he was flying, but suggested that he got off a little before the plane reached the airport, as it was possible the police there would search his plane. So he dropped the man in a field a little before the plane reached the main airport. Sure enough, when he landed at Warsaw, the police was already there to make a search for the man.

Soon thereafter, there was the Second World War. Poland was occupied by Germany. Tursky flew to England and there joined the R.A.F., and became a war-hero. He was a brave man, and after destroying a number of enemy planes, his own plane was hit. It crash-landed. The rescue party arrived there but found Tursky more dead than alive.

He was shifted to the nearest hospital. The doctors despaired of him and hesitated to operate on him. The next day, newspapers flashed the news of Tursky's accident. Tursky was in a state of coma. However, when he recovered, he found a short man looking at him through bright eyes. "Do you remember me?" he asked Tursky. "I was the one whom you saved. This morning I read the news that you were in a state of coma, hanging between life and death, and immediately I flew here."

"What for?" asked Tursky.

"Because," the man answered, "I thought I might be of help. They say that I am one of the best brain surgeons. I came here, and performed the operation which has saved your precious life."

When you do good, remember that good will return to you. The evil you do remains with you!

FATE AND FREE WILL

The question now arises: is man a free agent? Or is he a puppet in the hands of Destiny? Can he change his own fate?

Let me quote a saying I hear very often:

Bani banayi baan rahi aur kuch banani nah.

There are some people who will tell you everything is already 'written', that you cannot change what is to happen. Whatever you do, whatever efforts you put in, you will not be able to change your destiny.

There are others who tell you, that man is endowed with a free will, man has the freedom to change his destiny at every step, in every round of life.

Let me repeat the two different answers given to our question. The first is that man is a prisoner of his own fate. No matter how valiant his efforts, he cannot change the contours of his destiny.

The second answer is that man is absolutely free. He has the freedom of choice to act – to choose right or wrong. At every step of life, he can make the effort to improve his condition. Through his actions, he can actually succeed in changing his own *karma* and thus altering his own destiny.

I think that these two aspects of man's condition are like the twin blades of a pair of scissors. The first *karma* is *ichcha shakti* – the freedom of choice; the second is *prarabdha karma* – our accumulated *karma*. Only when the two go together, can we act in any sense of the term. When the two blades act together, the scissors does its job. You cannot cut a piece of cloth with just one blade of the scissors. Likewise, fate and free will are both necessary for action.

Karma determines so many things that you cannot change. *Karma* determines the type of family into which you are born, your religion, your race and the type of body in which you are born. These are things you cannot change.

I heard of a woman who spent lakhs of rupees to change the shape of her nose. The shape was changed through plastic surgery – but it was not to her satisfaction.

There was a man who spent a fortune, trying to increase his height by a couple of inches. He could not achieve this; his height could not be increased even by one millimetre.

But there is a place for free will even in such cases. Whatever be your fate, you always have this choice – of reacting to your fate in a positive or negative manner. This is always within your power!

ARE ALL MEN EQUAL?

People often ask me: Why is it that all men are not born equal? My answer is – Yes, all men are created equal.

No one can be so blind or foolish as to imagine that there is actual equality of ability or environment or conditions of birth for all. We all know that in the same family, all children do not have equality of ability or intelligence. There is a family I know of which the eldest son is an IAS officer, while the youngest is unable to pass his High School Board Examination!

We have a proverb in Sindhi which says, "The mother gives birth to children, each brings with himself his own destiny." In other words, each one brings his *karma* with himself. There is a family of which the youngest son is a multimillionaire, while the eldest is so poor that he and his children are virtually starving, literally begging for food.

Two questions arise:

1. Is this inequality the result of *karma*?
2. If it is so, is it fair?

The answer to both, as the great rishis have taught us, is in the affirmative. You are the architect of your own destiny. You are the builder of your own fate. Every thought, emotion, wish and action creates *karma*. We have been creating *karma* for millions, perhaps billions of years. If our thoughts, emotions and actions are benevolent, so-called good *karma* results. If they are malevolent, evil or difficult, bad *karma* is created.

The good or evil we generate attaches its effect to us and remains in our life-current until we have satisfied it by balancing it out.

The question then arises: if all that happens to us today is the result of our past *karma*, does it not imply that everything is pre-destined? That God leaves nothing to us to make our own lives better?

This, as we have seen earlier, is not true. Many of us may blame fate, *kismet,* for our misfortunes. But we are the architects of our own destiny, the builders of our own fate.

Scholars who have reflected on the cause-and-effect concept of *karma* explain it thus: any thought, word or action that emanates from us, brings with itself its adjunct, its accompanying impressions that are lodged in our mind as *samskaras.*

These *samskaras* - known as *karmic* residues – have the power to bring about our joy or sorrow in the future. These are further divided into two types depending upon their maturation: that is to say, some causes produce their effect immediately, while others take effect after a long time. Some of our actions bear fruit in this lifetime; some will come to fruition in another lifetime.

So far from being blind and pre-destined, this aspect of *karma* gives all of us the hope of salvation and liberation. When we become aware that our destiny is created by our own thoughts, words, actions and desires, then there is always the possibility that is open to us, to correct and improve ourselves by changing our thoughts and actions for the better! Thus, the sinner of today can become the saint of tomorrow just as today's pauper can work hard to become tomorrow's business tycoon. The mighty law of *karma* makes this possible for us all!

CHANGE YOUR *KARMA*!

The concept of 'pre-ordination' adhered to by a few orthodox theologians, holds that God settles and fixes the destiny of a man even before he is born into the world. This is neither logical, nor tenable. It makes man a puppet, a thing of straw, and, what is worse, it makes God partial, whimsical, unfair and unjust. Man's freedom of choice, his sense of moral responsibility and his independence are all nullified. Why should God make some of us rich, powerful and successful, while some of us are condemned to poverty, illness and despair? Why should we punish thiefs and cheats and murderers if they are pre-ordained to be as such, and are not responsible for their own actions?

Questions like these – and many more – will remain unanswered if we accept the theory of pre-ordination. On the other hand, the Doctrine of *karma* is lucid and clear: everyone reaps the fruits of his or her own actions. We can make or mar our destiny by our thoughts and actions. We are free agents; we are blessed with free will. We are free to choose between the two alternatives of good and evil, at every step, every turn of life.

The doctrine of *karma* is thus essentially one of hope and encouragement. It is the best motivation we can have for right thinking, right action and right living. If only we understood this law in its fullness, our lives would be beautiful indeed! We would learn the virtues of peace and contentment. We would bear the burdens of life with patience and acceptance. People would rejoice even in suffering.

God has created a universe of beauty, fullness, happiness and harmony. Each one of us is a child of God. God wishes each one of us to be happy, healthy, prosperous, successful and to enjoy all the good things he has created. We deny ourselves these bounties, only because of our *karma*. Change your *karma* and you will change the conditions in which you live!

MORE ABOUT *KARMA*

Karma is the word that is much used and abused today. We hear it all the time on TV. People say "It is my karma; I must have done something bad in the past", or "I am sure that my success is the effect of my good *karma*." I am told that in a school in the US, a history teacher told her students: "If you do good deeds, you will be reborn richer and higher. If you are bad, you will come back as a plant or a bug!"

We have to set the record straight, in the face of such misinterpretation. *Karma* in its original form means just "action". When something happens to us that is apparently unjust or unfair, it is not as if God is punishing us. Rather, it is the result of our own past actions.

The *Vedas* tell us that if we sow goodness, we will reap goodness; if we sow evil, we will reap evil. In other words, we are creating our own destiny by our thoughts, words and deeds.

Karma is the universal principle of cause and effect. The good that we do now, will bring us good in the future. The evil that we do, will equally accrue to our own destiny. *Karma* is the law, the divine system of justice that operates on human lives. The divine law tells us: whatever the condition we face now in our life, is the effect of our own past actions. Even bad *karma*, when faced in the spirit of acceptance and wisdom, can lead to spiritual growth. *Karma* is not God's code of punishment. It is the underlying principle that helps us to learn our lessons from the school of life, and 'pass out' as better human beings.

Some scholars compare *karma* to energy. We create energy through our thoughts, words and deeds – and in time, this energy comes back to us, may be through other people. *Karma* has also been compared to the law of gravity, for it acts equally upon us all. The law of *karma* is not passive on defeatist. It puts man at the center of responsibility for all that he does and all that is done to him.

Many people equate karma with evil, sin – whatever is bad. This is probably because we become aware of *karma* only when we face difficult situations. We take all good things in life for granted, of course!

Some people equate *karma* with fate or destiny – a pre-ordained destiny over which we have no control. This too, is as false as Karl Marx's claim that "Religion is the opium of the masses." There is no place for such negativism in the *Sanatana Dharma*. The Hindu Faith does not operate on fear psychosis, or by appeal to guilt or shame.

Let me explain with a simple example. Someone utters kind words to you – and you feel peaceful, happy and relaxed. Another person utters harsh, unkind words – and you are disturbed and upset. The kindness and harshness will return to the people who caused them – may be, at a later time.

Karma is thus, a natural law of the mind. We generate our own *karma* with our thoughts, words and deeds. It would be quite true to say that our thoughts create our *karma* – good, bad or indifferent!

INTIMATIONS OF IMMORTALITY

Many scholars and philosophers believe firmly, that when we are born into this world, we still carry with us beautiful visions of Heaven which is our true home, as well as memories of our past births which are deeply embedded in our soul. In this state of grace, our souls are radiant, and we are invested with a boundless capacity to give and receive love, to radiate joy and peace, and to experience true bliss.

Have you seen babies smile beautifully in their sleep? Have you seen the faraway look in their eyes, as they seem to see through you into eternity? This is a sign, that as very young infants, we carry with us visions of immortality.

The poet, William Wordsworth, captured this truth beautifully in his poem *Ode To Immortality* from which the title of this section is taken. Wordsworth says:

> Our birth is but a sleep and a forgetting:
> The Soul that rises with us, our life's Star,
> Hath had elsewhere its setting,
> And cometh from afar:
> Trailing clouds of glory do we come
> From God, who is our home:
> Heaven lies about us in our infancy!

Babies are truly in a state of joy and grace. They are truly like the lilies of the field: they toil not, nor do they fear. They do not worry about the past or the future. They are secure in the present moment.

Alas, the assault on our minds, hearts and emotions begins very early. Our inborn grace, our memories of the life of our soul, are suppressed by worldly influences. The spotless state of our soul is soon clouded by the indoctrinations of the world. Sad to say, even our parents, teachers, elders, the society we live in, inculcate wrong, false values in us. We are taught to love money, power, pleasure – all the shadow shapes of this world of *maya* (illusion).

There is a beautiful story in which we are told that a mother sees her three-year old son, bending low over the cradle of his newborn baby brother. She goes closer to investigate what the boy is up to. She hears him whisper in the baby's ears, "You must tell me about God and Heaven. I'm afraid I'm beginning to forget it all!"

This is not at all fanciful. We have so much to learn from our children, before they forget it all. We have been children, in this life and in the many lives before this one. We too have forgotten! If we wish to attain liberation, we must remember! We must renounce the worldly indoctrination that only leads to grief, despair and misery! We must reclaim our capacity for joy and love!

Dr. Brian Weiss, a distinguished psychiatrist, tells us that he heard this incident from a young mother. The family's pet dog had just died, and she had come out of the room to make a phone call to the vet, to make arrangements for the interment of the dog's body.

When she returned to the room, she was startled to see that her two year-old son had wrapped up the dog from head to tail – with Band-Aid and butter!

"Why... why have you done this?" she stammered.

"Mommy, I'm just making sure he slides into heaven, smooth and fast," was the toddler's reply.

When she mentioned the incident to a friend, she was told that this was, in fact, the burial practice of ancient Egyptians. She was even shown a book, with the picture of a buried dog, which looked exactly like their dog! She concluded that her son had been an Egyptian in his previous birth.

Watch a child at play – his joy and spontaneity are infectious. As we grow, we forget how to have 'real fun' out of life.

KARMA IS AN OPPORTUNITY

A Western thinker writes:

> ... we have debts that must be paid. If we have not paid out these debts, then we must take them into another life... you progress only by paying your debts...

Debts that must be paid... that sums up the concept of *karma*. But I would add that *karma* is not a burden that you have to carry. It is also an opportunity to learn, a chance to practise love and forgiveness, a chance to learn lessons that are valuable to us. *Karma* offers us the chance to wipe our dirty slate clean, to erase the wrong doings of the past.

Karma is a uniquely Hindu concept. But its basic tenets are reflected in many religions. Thus, the Bible tells us, "What you sow, that is what you reap." And further, "God will render to every man according to his deeds." Judaism says, "He who is liberal will be enriched, he who waters will himself be watered."

I always say that people who hurt and kill in the name of religion, are killing their own brethren, for the surest way to reincarnate in a particular race or religion, is to hate that particular religion. It has truly been said that religious hatred and intolerance will become like the express train that will carry you into the religion you hate!

Karma is an opportunity to learn; *Karma* is an opportunity to evolve spiritually; *karma* is an opportunity to repay all outstanding debts, so that we may be free to move onward, Godward!

HOW TO CREATE GOOD *KARMA*

It is easy for many of us to appreciate the principle of *karma* and to analyse it in philosophical terms. But we must also learn to cultivate the ability to master the working of *karma* in our daily lives, so that we create our own good *karma*. Here are a few principles that may help you in this regard.

Forgive and forget:

Revenge and retaliation are best left to time. Let us, in the words of the Lord's prayer, 'forgive those who trespass against us.' The impulse to take revenge only leads to negative *karma*. As Mahatma Gandhi observed, "The law of an eye for an eye makes the whole world blind."

Learn to be responsible for your thoughts, words and actions:

We must accept the responsibility for all that happens to us. We always practise this perfectly, when good things happen to us. If I stand first in an examination, I am happy to take all the credit. If my business prospers, I attribute it to my hard work and sagacity. But what if I am faced with troubles and difficulties? What, when the going is rough?

If we continue to 'pass the buck', blame others for our failures and troubles, we only accumulate negative *karma*. Instead, we must learn to accept the responsibility for our own destiny, and sow the seeds of good *karma*.

Refrain from causing pain to others:

When we harm others, we are paving the way for harming ourselves in the future! We will do well to pause before we act in anger, and reflect upon the consequences of our action.

Seek guidance from your Guru, or a spiritual elder:

Most of us lack the mental and spiritual strength to wage the battle of life alone. But the wonderful thing is we are not alone! Divine guidance for divine grace is always available to those who seek it. Turn to your guru or to a spiritual teacher who will help you overcome negative *karmic* patterns.

Do all that you can to mitigate the effect of past karma:

Not only must we accumulate good *karma* for the future, we must also rid ourselves of the effect of past *karma*. This may be compared to the judicial process by which a prisoner is released from confinement early, before his full sentence expires, on account of his good behaviour.

While it is true that we carry upon us the burden of our past *karma*, the negative effects of the burden can be mitigated to a large extent by our good deeds in this life.

Work towards your own liberation:

Many of us are apt to imagine that liberation from the bonds of *karma*, freedom from the cycle of birth and death, is not attainable for the likes of us. This is a defeatist, pessimistic attitude. Why wait for successive births, when liberation is possible for us sooner? When we set our sights firmly on the goal, we accelerate the pace of our own spiritual evolution. This is achieved through *bhakti* (devotion), *seva* (service) and *sadhana* (practice of austerities like meditation).

By consciously setting out to purify ourselves thus, we can accelerate the process of our own karma and get closer to *mukti* (liberation).

WE CREATE OUR OWN DESTINY

A Zen Master, Yun ku-hui tells us, "Fate is created by ourselves, our form is created by our mind, by our thoughts. Good luck or bad luck is also determined by ourselves."

Zen philosophy also teaches us that one can change one's destiny by "accumulating merit" – i.e. doing as many good deeds as one can. First, one should correct all bad habits as well as bad thought patterns.

The Zen Masters even have a score sheet of merits and demerits. Merits are the points we score, when we perform good deeds; demerits are minus points which take away our merits. Thus people set themselves the task of accumulating three thousand merits or ten thousand merits, in order to achieve the desired change in their lives.

There was an imperial official called Yuan, who once vowed to accumulate ten thousand merits for the sake of begetting a son. Soon thereafter, he became the Mayor of a district, where the taxes were very high. To help the poor farmers in the area, he decided to reduce the tax by half. This was a tough decision, but he went ahead with it boldly, and he was told that atleast ten thousand poor farmers in his district had benefited from the decision. With one stroke, he had indeed accumulated ten thousand merits, and a son was soon born to him.

There was a lady who belonged to the pious Lin family. Every day she would make rice balls to give to the poor.

However many pieces people asked for, she would give it to them.

There was a Tao monk who asked for six or seven rice balls everyday. He continued to come to her house for three years. She gave him whatever he asked for, without once expressing displeasure. Such was her sincerity and kindness that the Tao monk said to her, that future generations of the family would benefit from her generosity. "The number of your decedents who will prosper in life will be equivalent to the number of seeds in a pound of sesame seeds." True enough, her decedents flourished and grew prosperous.

Here are the ten methods recommended by Zen Master Liao–Fan Yuan:

- Benefit others in all that you do. Think about the welfare of all.
- Treat people with respect and love, no matter who they are and what they do.
- Help others, provide them with opportunity to do good.
- Encourage others, inspire others by your example, to do good.
- Help people in misfortune.
- Support public works that are meant for public good.
- Give of your material wealth generously.
- Protect and support all spiritual teaching.
- Respect your elders.
- Protect all forms of life.

As we all know, China is a vast and populous nation. For centuries together, before the Maoist Revolution, peace and harmony had always prevailed among her people. How was this possible in a vast land, where the Emperor lived too far away from most of the people to rule the people in a direct and effective way? The answer is clear. The understanding that "you reap what you sow" is deeply ingrained in the Chinese consciousness. The Chinese version of this saying is: "You harvest squash when you plant the seeds of squash, and you harvest beans when you plant the seeds of beans."

There was a woman named Yen, who lived in China in the olden days. The man who was later to become the father of Confucius, the great Chinese philosopher, asked for the hand of Yen's daughter in marriage. In reply, she only wished to know one thing: "Have your ancestors accumulated merit and virtue? I do not care if they are wealthy or not, but if they have accumulated merit, your offspring would be outstanding."

THE TWO SELVES WITHIN YOU

Have you heard the story of the man who had two wives? One was old – nearer to him in age, while the second was much younger. The younger one wanted her husband to appear young. So, whenever she saw a grey hair on his head, she would pull it out, day after day.

The first wife, on the other hand, was anxious that *she* should not appear to be older than her husband. And so, she took to the habit of pulling out some of his black hair, day after day. She was convinced that this would make him appear mature and respectable.

The result? The man soon lost all the hair on his head, becoming bald before he was fifty years of age!

There are two 'selves' within us, the higher and the lower. The higher nature impels us to overcome all that is negative in us – like greed, envy, anger and hatred – but the lower nature is inclined to suppress all that is positive, and lead us towards evil. The human soul is torn between these two conflicting forces of good and evil. It is only when we strengthen the positive forces within us, and identify with our higher self, that we can attain God-realization.

People are apt to boast today that we live in the Age of Computers – the Age of Science and Technology. The world is full of infinite possibilities, they claim. The sky is the limit for all our aspirations!

Science and technology cannot solve all the ills that torment mankind. Do we not have illness, poverty, pain and misery in this planet, even now?

When scientists succeeded in splitting the atom, they rejoiced that they had discovered the means to create abundant energy and power, but what happened was something horrible. This secret of splitting the atom was misused and abused, to rain death and destruction on Hiroshima and Nagasaki.

We now know that science and technology can be used for good or bad purposes. It is only when we use it wisely and well that it can truly be a blessing to humanity.

So it is with our lives. It is only when we will live consciously, vigilantly, aware of everything we say and do, that we can achieve good *karma*. We need to act with wisdom, enlightenment and balance.

TYPES OF *KARMA*

As we sow, so we reap – this is a universal law, which applies to all planes of existence. Every wrong thought or impulse is a seed we sow in the subconscious mind; this impulse forms an impression; this impression is nurtured and grows into an act. Every act we perform has an effect on our life. Thus it is through our past actions, our past *karma* that we are moulded into a complex of *gunas - sattva, rajas* and *tamas.* From this complex of *gunas* is inherited our nature, or *swabhava.* We act, and we react to situations according to our nature or *swabhava.* The nature of our work, our role in life, our duty – *swadharma* – is determined by our *swabhava.*

All actions performed in the true spirit of *dharma* or righteousness contribute to the peace, harmony, balance and integrity of our lives. All action pertaining to *adharma* produces disorder, disharmony and strife. Thus is Cosmic justice rendered, and the scales of the Universe held even.

In order to understand this balance of cosmic justice, it is necessary for us to grasp three different aspects – three different types of *karma*:

1.   The first type of *karma* is *kriyaman* or *agami karma.* This is the *karma* of action and instant reaction. For example, you are thirsty and you drink water. Drinking water is an effort, an action. It produces an effect immediately – your thirst is quenched. The reaction cancels out the action and

the *karma* is settled, on the spot; there is no residue to be carried over. *Kriyaman karma* is that which cancels itself there and then. You take a bath; it is an action by which your body is cleansed; this is the effect which is immediately achieved. Causes subside, when the effect is produced. Action comes to an end, when the reaction sets in. Thus, *kriyaman karma* is not carried forward. Any action of yours that leads to immediate result is *kriyaman karma*. Action and reaction – *kriya* and *pratikriya* are both completed; they have no effect on your future actions.

2. The second is *sanchita karma*, the sum total and store of all our actions, good and bad in the sequence of innumerable lives that we have lived. All of this is recorded and preserved.

I repeat, *sanchita karma* is the *karma* that we have accumulated through numerous lives. All the actions we have performed – physical, mental, vocal – contribute to create this store house of *karma*. However, all this *karma* does not fructify, does not bear fruit at once. Only a small part of it fructifies in any one birth or embodiment. The rest of it remains accumulated – awaiting its fructification.

Let me give you a simple example. You appear for an examination: you do not get the result immediately. You have to wait for two or three months – in some cases, up to six months before your results are declared. So, your appearing for an exam becomes a sort of *sanchita karma*, which does not produce its effect immediately,

Karma which does not fructify immediately, *karma* which does not produce its effect immediately is *sanchita karma*. Our *sanchita karma* keeps on growing; in fact it grows from birth to birth; it has been accumulating on a spiritual record through innumerable lives from time immemorial. The load of *sanchita karma* which each one of us carries is tremendous – indeed, a heavy load! All those *karmas* which do not produce their effect immediately are held in deposit – they are added to our accounts of *karma*.

I remember, a few years ago, the Sadhu Vaswani Mission had instituted a prize to be awarded to anyone who could recite the 700 *slokas* of the Bhagavad Gita by heart. So far, no one has come to claim this prize. The amount is still lying in deposit. It is a *sanchita prize*.

We saw the example of King Dashratha earlier. While he was hunting, he accidentally killed Shravan Kumar, whose blind parents were grief stricken at their loss and cursed him; just as they had been afflicted by separation from their son, and were to die of grief, the killer of their son too, would face a similar fate, in times to come. Now this curse could not take effect immediately, because Dashratha was not married. So this *karma* was in deposit, part of *sanchita karma* - until that fatal day on which Rama was to be crowned as king, and Kaikeyi came to ask for the implementation of the two boons he had promised her earlier. We know how the curse was fulfilled, and king Dashratha died due to the grief of separation from his beloved son, Sri Rama.

Sanchita karma is *karma* that waits for an opportunity. It emphasises the law that you cannot get away with anything. Let us suppose that there is a person who has borrowed a lakh rupees from you, and is unable to give it back to you: you go to a court of law and you get a decree against him. The bailiff goes to execute the decree, but finds that the man is bankrupt – he has no money to pay you. In such a case, the decree is not cancelled; it is kept pending. As soon as this man earns money, the decree will be executed against him.

Let us imagine however, that this man dies before your loan has been repaid. The whole world would say, "He's been let off the hook," or "He got away with it after all!" Well, he may have been let off from the point of view of the world; for indeed, our worldly courts can do nothing further with him – but his *karma* will not let him get away with it. The money that he owed to you, the money that he failed to repay, becomes part of his *sanchita karma*. In some future birth or births, he will have to repay this amount to you in the form of money or service. He may even be born as a bullock or an ox on your farm, so that he may pay off his debt through labour. The law of *karma* as I said, is emphatic on this point. You cannot get away with anything!

We saw too, the story of King Dritarashtra, who demanded to know of Lord Krishna why God had afflicted him with blindness. With his yogic power, he could look back over one hundred previous births of his - and he could see that he had performed no such bad *karma* which would result in blindness. Then it was that Lord Krishna helped him go back even further; and he saw that several births earlier, he had blinded a swan and killed all its hundred signets. As a result, he was now born blind, and lost his hundred sons, the Kauravas.

Ever since we first take human birth, action and reaction go on, and our *karma* accumulates. Some people perform negative actions, actions of *adharma*, yet they do not seem to reap the fruits of their bad actions. However, their bad *karma* lies latent, waiting to bear fruit. Similarly, the good *karma* of people who have performed virtuous actions may also be lying latent. One day, in some future birth, they will surely bring their reward.

3. The third type of *karma* is that part of our *karma* which matures, comes to fruition in one particular birth. This is *prarabdha karma*, and it is this *karma* which is the basis of our present birth, our present embodiment. Those of us who have been given the gift of human birth, we may

be sure that this is the result of very good *karma*. Thus *prarabdha karma* on which our present existence is based, is often referred to as fate, destiny or luck, in popular language.

Prarabdha karma is a part, or a fragment of *sanchita karma* which has fructified in this birth. Our *sanchita karma*, accumulated over hundreds of births, is like a mountain; and in each *janma*, we are adding to the store. Of this vast store, the *prarabdha* – the inevitable – is but a fragment. It is that portion of our *karma* assigned to us to be worked out in our present existence. It is also called ripe *karma*, for it is a debt which has become overdue, and must be paid back.

It is *prarabdha karma* which determines the family into which you are born. It determines the race, the nation in which you take birth; it also determines your sex, the type of body you will acquire etc. Remember this – your wealth is pre-determined. You may keep working all day, all night to get more money – but only that much money will come to you, which is permitted by *prarabdha*. Even if you get more, you will lose it through speculation, theft, etc.

There was a young man whose parents refused to give him money for speculation in the share-market. He cursed himself, saying, "My greatest blunder is to have been born in this family."

Well, the young man may regard it as his blunder, but being born in a particular family is your *prarabdha karma*.

I know of another young man, who is short statured. For years, he has been at it, trying to increase his height. He has tried everything, from *ayurveda* to yoga – he has not added even one inch to his height. For this too, is determined by your *prarabdha*.

You must also remember, that for exhausting your *prarabdha karma*, you need a physical body. It is only in this physical body that you can exhaust your *prarabdha karma*. And until it is exhausted, you will not be able to drop this body. You may be bed-ridden for years together; you may be afflicted with paralysis, or with some other crippling disease; you may be praying every day for your deliverance, and your near and dear ones may be praying for your deliverance – but you will not be delivered until you have paid off, exhausted through suffering or through enjoyment, as may be the case, your *prarabdha karma*. It is only when this *prarabdha karma* is exhausted that your physical body will drop down, and you will get a period of freedom, until you wear another physical body – to work out more *karma* that may have fructified in the meanwhile.

Every day, every hour, we come across several instances of old people who are bed-ridden, unable to see, hear or move, praying desperately for deliverance from life. We hear, too, of old people who have lived hale and hearty lives, suddenly afflicted with terminal illnesses like cancer, when they are past the age of 90 or more. Sometimes, misguidedly, we may even think, "How cruel of God to let these old people suffer thus! They would be better off dead, rather than suffering like this!" Truly, their life has become an ordeal of suffering. Their frail and disease-stricken bodies are like prisons in which their immortal souls are trapped. In Western countries, they even discuss *'mercy killing'* (surely a contradiction in terms!) to end the life of patients suffering from incurable and terminal diseases. Oh, it would be an act of kindness to release them from the agony that life has become – so we think!

We could not be farther from truth! For our present life – our condition, our circumstances, even our longevity, are all determined by *prarabdha karma*. Until this is exhausted, – we cannot drop our physical bodies, however much we may long for release from the burden that life may have become. Indeed, our life will be prolonged – in some cases inexplicably; in some cases miraculously; in some cases against our own will – until every bit of our *prarabdha* is exhausted.

In total contrast to this, we also come across tragic deaths of the very young, including babies, small children and newly married couples. We grieve over such 'untimely' deaths – for they seemed to have a lifetime before them, and they have departed from this earth before they have experienced all that life had to offer to them. A tragic accident, a natural disaster, a sudden illness snatches them away, and we are not able to reconcile their loss. Someone who is fit and fine, suffers a massive cardiac arrest and dies instantly. School children, laughing and chatting gaily, are mowed down when their bus hits a train. The newspapers are full of such stories. "Why? Why?" we ask ourselves in bewilderment.

The answer is simple. Their fructified *karma* has been exhausted. The purpose for which they had to assume their physical body in *this* lifetime has been completed. Back their souls must return, to reap the rewards of this lifetime.

Not a day more or less, not a second more or less can we live upon this earth, than the duration of life that has been ordained to us by our own *prarabdha karma*. When we understand this, we will not be baffled by 'untimely' deaths or prolonged lives. Each soul must live out its allotted term upon this earth, until its fructifying *karma* lasts – until the fruit has been eaten, to the last sweet or bitter portion.

When I hear about the feuds between Hindus and Muslims, I am sometimes amused to think that some of these people who are fighting for Hinduism today, may actually have been Muslims in their previous birth! Equally, in a future birth, they may be reborn as Muslims! All these quarrels and feuds are meaningless – for your race and religion are also determined by your *prarabdha karma.* This 'destiny' is not something imposed on you from outside – you have built your own destiny through the efforts of yesterday. Yesterday's effort is today's destiny. Equally, today's effort is going to be tomorrow's destiny. Thus it is you yourself who are responsible for what is happening to you. The family into which you are born, your relatives, your friends, your spouse, your children, your religion, your race, your environment, your work, your wealth, the longevity of your life – all these are controlled by *prarabdha karma.*

There are a few important observations which I must make at this stage, with regard to the three types of *karma* that we have been discussing.

In any particular birth, while I am exhausting my *prarabdha karma,* the *karma* that has fructified, I am simultaneously creating new *karma.* I may exhaust in this birth, one hundred thousand *prarabdha karmas,* but in the process, I create millions of other *karmas,* and these are added to my store of *sanchita karma,* and thus it goes on...

THE WHEEL OF *KARMA*

The plight of man is sad indeed! Even while he is exhausting his *prarabdha karma*, he is adding to his store of *sanchita karma*, for he continues to sow the seeds of *karma* anew! Our *sanchita karma* keeps growing, and we live in ignorance of this inescapable truth! Unable to liberate ourselves from our own *karma*, we find ourselves ruthlessly trapped by our own actions. We consult astrologers and palmists to know of our future, little realising that it is our past and present actions that determine our future!

I am reminded of the condition of some of our poor village folk, a century or so ago. When they were in desperate need, these poor peasants would borrow money from the village money-lender. It might be for a happy event like a marriage in the family, or childbirth; or to provide treatment to someone who was ill. Whatever the cause, the money-lender would gladly advance the amount to them.

"Here I offer you one thousand rupees," the money-lender would say. "You will have to pay me only forty rupees per month by way of interest."

The peasant, in his ignorance would be very pleased. After all, what is forty rupees per month? Just a little more than one rupee a day! He would be satisfied that the rate of interest was indeed very reasonable. He could not calculate the interest; therefore, he would never realise that he was actually paying 48% interest on his loan!

The money lender, for his part, would pass on the loan to the villager after deducting the first six months interest. So Rs 240 would be deducted to start with, and the villager would receive just Rs. 760 in hand, for which he would be required to pay Rs. 40 every month by way of interest. If perchance, he failed to pay the interest on time, it would be added to his capital amount, and the interest would be calculated anew. And so it would go on accumulating. The villager would never be able to pay back his loan during his lifetime!

This is what happens to us with our *sanchita karma*. It keeps on multiplying by leaps and bounds. It is not possible for us to exhaust it entirely. And so we are mercilessly bound to this wheel of *karma*, this wheel of birth and death.

The *puranas* tell us a memorable tale of a king who wished to control his own future destiny. He approached a saint and said to him, "O Holy One! You are a *trikaal gnani* – the past, the present and the future hold no secrets from you. I beg you to tell me what the future holds in store for me."

"Tell me, O King," said the saint, "what do you hope to gain from knowledge of your future?"

"If I know the worst that can happen to me, surely I can take steps to prevent the inevitable, the untoward incidents that may befall me," the King replied.

"If I tell you, King," the saint warned, "try as you might, you cannot prevent that which is to happen."

"I beg to differ," the King retorted. "If I know the worst, you and I together can work to prevent harm befalling me. Between us, we will surely find a way."

"So be it," said the saint. "I shall now begin to relate the events of your future. And with it, I offer you this challenge – you cannot prevent what is to happen, however hard you may try."

"Let me begin with this moment. Today is Thursday. Next Wednesday, someone will present you with a magnificent horse. I request you now, *not* to accept the horse for any reason. But I also tell you, you will not be able to refuse it. You will accept it.

"The next day, you will ride the horse into the forest, reaching where the road runs in two directions. I warn you here and now, *do not* turn left; take the right turn. But I know that you will take the left turn and ride farther.

"Down the road, you will come across a beautiful woman, in deep distress and sorrow, who will implore you for help. I must urge you, O King, *not* to take pity on this woman, not even to cast a glance in her direction, and simply ride on. But I know for certain that you will not heed this warning. You will alight from the horse to offer help to the woman.

"Having offered to help the distressed woman, let me implore you to go further. *Do not* allow her charms to ensnare you. However, I know that you will not be able to resist her beauty. You will take her with you and make her your queen.

"Soon thereafter, the queen will get you to perform a special *yagna*. O King, *by no means* must you consent to her wishes and undertake to perform the *yagna*. But alas, I know that you will go ahead and do exactly as she says.

"During the *yagna*, a young Brahmin will appear before you and seek your permission to participate in the proceedings. Having ignored my warnings all along, King, pay heed to this one at least – *do not* grant permission to this young man to take part in the *yagna*.

"Alas, he will go ahead and participate in your *yagna*. In the course of the *yagna*, he will begin to mock at you and your queen. I warn you, O King, to guard your temper at that juncture, for your own good.

"I know for certain, that *you will fail* to control your anger, and in a fit of rage, you will kill the young Brahmin. And the terrible sin of *brahmahatya* will alight on you! And your strong and handsome body will be covered with leprous sores! You will be liberated from this predicament when you hear the story of the *Mahabharata* with deep reverence and devotion.

"I have spoken," concluded the saint, "and I have warned you of the dangers. But you *cannot* escape your *Karma*."

The king grew thoughtful, and was determined to heed the saint's warnings at every juncture that was crucial. Forewarned is fore-armed, he thought to himself. With prior knowledge, he felt he would be able to alter events and circumstances.

Everything came to pass, just as the saint had predicted. Such was the power of his *prarabdha karma*, that at no point was the king able to act as per the saint's instructions. At each turn, he made the wrong decision. Events followed one another, until the prognosticated *yagna* came about, and the young Brahmin provoked him beyond endurance. In a desperate, last ditch effort, the king tried to control his rage. But failing utterly, he killed the young Brahmin in a fit of rage, contracting the dreaded sin of *brahmahathya*.

The effect of *prarabdha karma* then, is inescapable, no matter how hard we try to evade its consequences. Only two choices are open to us – to accept whatever happens in a spirit of faith, and to bear it cheerfully; or to resist it, protest against our fate and spend our life in misery. We cannot change our *prarabdha karma* – but we can, in fact we must change our attitude to life.

The question therefore arises: is there a way out for us?

After all, a day comes in the life of everyone, when he wants to be freed. The wheel of birth and death is not a wheel of eternal happiness! We are only too well aware that

while we get a little pleasure, we also undergo a great deal
of agony, anguish, misery and suffering. At such times, we
cry for relief: Is there a way out? Is there a way out? How
may we find the way? How may we be freed once and for
all, from this load of *karma*?

FREEDOM THROUGH DIVINE GRACE

We have said that we are bound by the law of *karma*, and that our personality, our present life, and even our *swabhava* or nature, are determined by our past *karma*. This will make you wonder whether your own effort or voluntary action has anything to do with your liberation. After all, if everything is pre-determined, what is the use of human effort?

In one of our ancient texts, the *Yoga Vashishta,* Sri Rama's guru, sage Vashishta, assures him that self-effort can lead to liberation, that man has infinite freedom to achieve his liberation through self-effort. How is this possible, given the nature of *sanchita* (stored) *karma* and *prarabdha* (fructifying) karma?

There are several scholars who argue that *prarabdha karma* does not determine every aspect and every detail of our present lives. Rather, *prarabdha* represents only the broad outline of this, our present life – like our family background, the general circumstances of our life, our broad personality traits, and certain crucial events in our life.

While this is given, they argue, *purushartha* or self-effort can always help you improve upon this broad outline.

Let me give you an example. If *prarabdha* has made you wealthy and prosperous in this life, you will waste it all away if you remain idle and complacent, simply revelling in wordly pleasures. On the other hand, if you cultivate humility and compassion through your self-effort, you are actually improving upon your *prarabdha*. You will then give freely to the poor and the needy, and devote your God-given wealth to the service of your fellow human beings. Thus, you are ensuring that your past good *karma* is actually being converted to good *karma* for your future!

Let us say, on the other hand, that you are in a state of poverty because of your *prarabdha karma*. Your business fails; you struggle to succeed – but in vain. What do you do – give up the struggle and live in misery and frustration? Of course not! Read the life-stories of the world's millionaires, and you will know that they struggled till they overcame adversity and failure. True, many of us struggle to make ends meet, without ever becoming millionaires. But then, our adversity has been put to good effect; through our self-effort, we learn the virtues of patience, perseverance, tolerance and determination. So, no matter what *prarabdha* brings us, our self-effort can help us improve upon it.

The ancient scriptures of India tell us that there are four objectives for self-effort – four purposes of life. These have been identified as *dharma*, *artha*, *kama* and *moksha*.

Dharma represents the ethical qualities of one's life. These moral values should form the basis of all our actions. If our actions are unethical or immoral, all that we achieve in life will have no real meaning or value. Take a man, who has built up a fortune by deceit and fraud and corruption. The pomp and show of his lifestyle is like a moth-eaten structure. So too, with a society or a nation, which believes only in material progress at any cost. Such a society is likely to disintegrate with moral degeneration. Thus *dharma* must be the basis of all our self-effort.

The second objective, *artha*, represents material values. Our ancestors were not impractical to overlook the importance of material security. We must strive in order to have the means for our livelihood. We do not have to be millionaires, but we must have enough means to fulfill all the duties that *dharma* demands of us.

The third objective, *kama*, represents the vital value of desire. *Kama* motivates us to make friends, to marry and start a family, to relate to the people around us. Within the bounds of dharma, *kama* can lead to a life of joyous fulfilment.

However, all these values – *dharma, artha* and *kama* are but means to an end. The ultimate goal of human life is *moksha* or liberation – and this requires untiring, unfailing, persistent self-effort from us. Liberation is not determined by destiny; liberation cannot be predicted by astrology or palmistry. Liberation is achieved only through self-effort and the grace of God or the Guru.

In this process, you will need the guidance of a guru, whose moral support can help you on the path. Self-effort is necessary to surrender your will to the guru, and to pursue the path with faith and devotion.

When you follow the right direction, you will soon realise that you are being drawn towards Divine grace. Your self-effort has led you to this beautiful state, which is the ultimate aim of human life.

Many people are often confused about the balance between self-effort and Divine grace. What is the dividing line between the two? Does self-effort cease when Divine grace operates?

Let us take the case of an unemployed youth. He is trying hard to get himself a job. One day, he reads a book on Divine grace. Can he sit back and tell himself, "I shall sit back and give up. Divine grace will surely find a job for me"?

All of us know Divine grace sustains our life. Yet none of us sits still before a plate of food and wait for divine grace to bring the food to our lips!

In this, as in so many other things, we operate on double standards. When there is something that we desire intensely – like the first rank in class, the first prize in a contest, or a girl/boy we love – we put in every effort to secure the object of that desire. When we encounter obstacles in our path, we invoke Divine grace. When we don't get what we want, we deny the mercy of God.

This is not the right attitude: as the saying goes, God helps those who help themselves. God's grace operates through your own mind, intellect and heart. God's grace guides your every effort, though you may be unaware of it. As you strive to do the best you can, Divine grace prompts you, supports you at every step.

Our scriptures distinguish four aspects of Divine grace – *Ishwara kripa*, *Guru kripa*, *Shastra kripa* and *Sva kripa*.

Ishwara kripa is the Divine assistance that comes to our aid when all else fails us. Consider the plight of Draupadi, as she was about to be disgraced, dishonoured, de-robed by the Kauravas. King Dritarashtra did nothing to stop the dastardly deed of his sons; the Kuru elders, Bhishma, Drona, Kripa were powerless in the face of such evil; as for her five husbands, they bowed down their heads in utter humiliation and shame. All earthly sources of help failed Draupadi utterly, in her hour of desperate, piteous need.

However, Draupadi knew that there was One whose grace is unfailing. One, whose support is perennial. Therefore, she called upon Sri Krishna. He came to her aid promptly.

We have all benefited from *Ishwara kripa* in our lives, though circumstances might not have been so dramatic.

Think of such occasions as this – when you narrowly escaped a fall, or a motor accident; when you missed a train or a flight, and learnt later that it met with a crash/disaster. It is God's grace that saved you, though we acknowledge this only on rare occasions and during momentous events.

Guru kripa or the grace of the guru, is the amazing protection that the guru offers to his disciples. When we surrender ourselves to his will utterly and completely, the guru's guidance is made available to us at every step.

Shastra kripa, the grace of the scriptures, is not obtained merely by reading the words or the pages of the sacred texts. It is when you approach the scriptures in the right frame of mind, with the right attitude, and eager to assimilate their truth, that their essential meaning is revealed to you. When you internalise the truth of the texts you read – and not merely quote or recite from them – you have reached a crucial stage in your spiritual development.

Sva kripa or the grace of your own soul enables you to take a deep interest in spiritual matters. You are not distracted by materialistic goals; worldly affairs do not take you away from the chosen path to God; you are not tempted by the passing shadows of life. The grace of the soul enables you to pursue the pilgrim-path with patience and perseverance.

All these four aspects represent Divine grace in different manifestations. We need to be receptive, to benefit from them. Like the quality of Mercy that Shakespeare spoke of, Divine mercy is "not strained"; it too, "droppeth as the gentle rain from heaven". Nowadays, we talk of rain-harvesting, which requires special efforts and specific arrangements. So too, if we are to receive Divine grace, we must learn to become willing receptacles of the same. This is possible through *sadhana* or spiritual discipline.

Sadhana too, is a matter of self-effort. Of course, this effort must not be tainted by egoism, greed or pride. But this becomes possible, when we realise the ever-loving presence of God in our lives, and surrender ourselves to this Grace. You realise then, the crucial inter-dependence between your effort and His Grace.

WHAT IS FATE?

What will be, will be...

Que Sera, Sera...

The lines of the popular song express the popular view of fate. Most of us regard fate as that mysterious, inescapable force that governs our future. "It is in the stars," we say, shifting responsibility to astrology. "It is written thus on my brow," we remark, absolving ourselves of all accountability.

True, it is fate that governs your future – but it is you who create your own destiny. You ordain your own fate, by the law of cause and effect.

God has given us the freedom to choose, the freedom to act. But we are responsible for the outcome of our own choices and actions. Thus every choice we make, every act we perform becomes a cause that will produce an effect. When you set in motion negative forces, you will generate negative effects. Whether we choose good or evil, we will reap the result of our choice. Thus, every day, every hour, every minute of our lives, we are creating the causes that will determine our fate and our future.

When a person is afflicted with a heart problem, he bemoans his fate. If only he would look carefully at his actions, he will realize he has been eating the wrong kind of food, leading the wrong kind of lifestyle and choosing bad habits over good ones. A bad lifestyle was the cause; the heart problem is the effect. He himself has created his 'fate'.

Disease or good health; success or failure; poverty or wealth; all these are the effects of causes we have created in our past. However, we can change the effect on our fate if we choose the right way through right action.

Let me give you an example. When we are ill, we go to a doctor. This is one way to *minimise, mitigate* the bad effects of our illness. However, when the disease is deep-rooted, the underlying cause has to be eliminated.

Another way to change fate is to *resist* the effects of our causes. Thus, when we are confronted by trouble, we can affirm our belief in the goodness of God, in the positive forces of health and happiness. In such a state of mind, the negative conditions will affect you far less than they otherwise would. Thus you create an environment that will prevent the fruition of your bad *karma.*

A third way to control your fate is to *break* the hold that fate has on you, to *stop* its bad effects completely. This involves a process like surgery, when a diseased organ is removed from our body.

Sri Krishna tells: "As fire reduces to ashes all wood, O Arjuna, so does the flame of wisdom consume all *karma.*" When you surrender the thread of your life in God's hands and meditate deeply, God's divine grace cauterises, burns, amputates all evil effects from your life.

Did not Jesus demonstrate that even death is alterable in the story of Lazarus? According to Lazarus's *karma* he died on a certain day. But Jesus worked a miracle, and brought him back to life.

Never give up your good efforts. They will definitely help you change, resist even stop your *karma.* You truly will become the Master of your own Fate.

CHANGE YOUR THOUGHTS – CHANGE YOUR DESTINY

As I have stressed repeatedly, man cannot interfere with his *karma* but he can surely change his attitude to life, and to all that befalls him.

Two girls appeared for an important examination. They could not do well in the papers. One of them became disconsolate; she was dejected at the thought of failure, and actually began to contemplate suicide. The other took a more pragmatic approach. "What is past is past," she said to herself. "My frustration, sighs and tears cannot now change the results of the examination. Let me therefore focus my efforts on what is to come." Then and there, she resolved to prepare for the next examination, working hard so that she might pass with flying colours. We all have the same freedom – to accept all that happens to us in the right spirit, and to concentrate our efforts on succeeding where it really matters. Attitude is thus of the utmost importance in our actions, reactions and responses.

Suppose you and your friend give away something in charity; your attitude will determine the fruit of your action. For instance, one of you might be doing the charitable act for the sake of exhibitionism, to show off his generosity to the world. The other might be giving whatever he can in the spirit of love and service. Obviously, the differing attitude will determine the resultant fruits of their *karma*.

Many people tell me, "Often we act in innocence, without any ulterior motives. Yet people accuse us of wrong intent. Who is responsible for the results of such actions?"

My answer to them is: If your intentions are pure and honourable, your actions will only lead to good. If your conscience is clear, you need not pay heed to what others say or think about you. When you act in the right spirit, only good will result from your actions.

PRACTICAL SUGGESTIONS

In the following pages, I offer you a few practical suggestions, which may help you live your life in witness to the Law of *Karma*.

The Law of *Karma* tells us to love all, to serve all, and to share all that you have with others. Do not covet what belongs to others. Do not slander or cast aspersions on others; do not speak ill of people behind their back. Do not cheat others – for you are only cheating yourself. For this is the law of life, the fraud you perpetrate on others will, one day affect you.

Here is the true story of an architect. He married the daughter of a millionaire. His father-in-law purchased an expensive plot of land on a picturesque hill, and requested the architect to build a beautiful bungalow for him on the plot.

"I am going abroad, and I will not be back for six months," he said. "I hope you will complete the construction of the bungalow by then. Spare no expenses! Use the best materials. Send all the bills to my office, and you will be reimbursed immediately."

The architect was not a man of integrity. "Here is my chance," he thought. "It is my own father-in-law who has commissioned the bungalow. All expenses will be paid and no questions asked. I shall make as much money as possible out of this project."

And so he used the cheapest and poorest quality of material to build the bungalow. Security, safety and durability were all ignored as the architect concentrated on falsifying the bills, and making money for himself. The bungalow was completed in record time. The architect took care to give the house a glossy, beautiful exterior finish – no one could guess that what lay underneath the gloss was a weak poor structure!

The millionaire returned home. The architect called on him to say that his dream-home was ready.

"Is it complete? That must be some kind of record!" exclaimed the father-in-law, delighted. "You know tomorrow is my daughter's – I should say your wife's – birthday. Tomorrow, the three of us shall go together to see the new house!"

The next day, the three of them went together to see the bungalow. The unsuspecting father was absolutely charmed by what he saw. It was indeed a magnificent bungalow that his son-in-law had built.

"I congratulate you on the excellent job you have done," he said, "and now, here is the surprise. This bungalow was not meant for my use. It is a gift to the two of you, on the happy occasion of my dear daughter's birthday!"

The architect was stunned. Here he was, so proud of having cheated his father-in-law of lakhs of rupees – while, in truth, he had been cheating himself! "How stupid and greedy I have been!" he thought ruefully. "All the cheap materials I used, the short cuts I took, and the poor construction that was meant to defraud my father-in-law! It has backfired on me!"

This is what happens to us when we try to deceive others. Our deception and fraud come home to roost on us. This is the inescapable Law of *Karma*, which we cannot manipulate or twist as we please.

Sometimes, we imagine that deeds that are done in the darkness of night, acts which we perform in stealth and secrecy are seen by no one. True it is, no human eyes see them. But each act, each word, each thought of ours is like a seed we are sowing in the field of life. As surely as day follows night, the seed will sprout, germinate, grow into a tree and bear fruit. Eat that fruit we must, whether it is bitter or sweet.

TAKE CARE OF YOUR THOUGHTS

There is a special type of deep meditation, entering into which man can look into his astral self, and actually become aware of his past *karma* – what seeds he has sown on the field of his life in previous births. These memories lie hidden, deep in our astral self.

Therefore, my first practical suggestion is, always take care of your thoughts. As you think, so you become. Be vigilant. Don't dismiss your thoughts lightly, as they come and go. Don't neglect your thoughts, for thoughts have tremendous power. Thoughts are forces, thoughts have form, shape and colour. Thoughts can be *satvic* or *tamasic*, and they lead us to action. Let us remove all negative thoughts from our minds, so that our lives may be pure. An effective way of pushing out a negative thought is to slap or pinch yourself the moment an undesirable thought enters your mind.

When my Beloved Master, Sadhu Vaswani, was studying in college, he always carried a safety pin with him. Whenever an unwanted thought crossed his mind, he would immediately prick himself with the pin, and in the sharp pain that arose, obliterate the bad thought there and then.

Prophet Mohammed has said that greed comes to us like a traveller, who knocks at the door of our hearts, begging humbly to be admitted within. If we allow it to enter, it quickly becomes our master and controls our lives, while we watch helplessly.

When undesirable thoughts and emotions arise within us, we must learn to shut the door on their face and tell them firmly that there is no room in our hearts for evil. If you like, you can even say aloud, "House Full!" All evil thoughts will then flee from you, even as thieves flee when the alarm is raised.

There is a technique recommended in *Raja yoga* for people who wish to cultivate good and right thinking. This is the practice of *pratipaksha bhavana*, or substitution of bad thoughts by good. This involves three steps :

    a. Detach yourself from your negative thoughts

    b. Substitute a positive thought in its place

    c. Sublimate the negative into the positive

Let us consider the example of a man who is prone to jealousy. When this ugly emotion raises its head in his heart he should try to detach himself from it and observe it as if he was an outsider. When one witnesses one's own thoughts thus, negative emotions cannot continue to rise.

Thus, the progress of the negative emotion is checked. Next, he must build up in his mind, a healthy, wholesome picture that is contrary to jealousy – a picture of love, compassion, understanding and harmony. The beauty and warmth of these good feelings will gradually permeate his thoughts, dispelling the darker emotions.

In the third stage, the man must make use of auto-suggestion, to tell himself that he is the embodiment of all that is good in the universe – peace, joy and love. This will definitely help him to sublimate negative feelings into a positive awareness of all that is good.

The final process of sublimation is vital. If our negative thoughts are not sublimated thus, they will merely remain suppressed and subsequently express themselves in undesirable actions. *Pratipaksha bhavana* can thus release all negative energies from our minds and reinforce us with positive energies.

It is a healthy practice to start the day with positive affirmations: I recommend the simple assertion, "By God's grace, every day, in every way, I am determined to become better and better." It is very useful too, to take up your favourite *mantra* or *shloka* and repeat it to yourself. This will also help to elevate your thoughts.

SAY NO TO NEGATIVE EMOTIONS

"As a man thinketh, so he becomes," is the immutable law of human nature. Fill your mind with thoughts of joy, love, peace and harmony; these aspects will be reflected in your life. Give way to fear and despair – you will sink into abject misery.

Modern management gurus talk of something which they call "negative self-fulfilling prophecy." If you think you are going to fail, you most probably will; if you are afraid of poverty, disease or accident, you will in all likelihood, encounter the same.

Fear is the source of despair and sin. Fearlessness by contrast, is the greatest virtue. When you conquer fear, you conquer your lower self.

Pessimism, the negative way of looking at life, is a highly destructive attitude. It is a sure joy-killer. It not only blights one's life, it is also a disease which its carriers transmit to others.

There was a couple who began to quarrel bitterly in the house of a friend. The friend was so upset by all the unpleasantness that he became utterly miserable. He went to bed in that frame of mind, and woke up with with a grim determination that he himself would never, ever marry.

Imagine his shock when he met the same couple the next day – they were happy, laughing, friendly and at peace. They had made up after their quarrel. But their negativism had been passed on to their poor friend!

One way to cultivate optimism is to be aware of the truth that there is a meaning of mercy in all that happens to us. You will promote optimism when you ask God to give you the wisdom to understand all that happens to you in the right spirit.

When you allow your subconscious to store negative feelings and emotions, you will find it very difficult to become positive and optimistic. Every time you give in to fear and despair, negative impressions gain the upper hand in your subconscious. You will constantly gravitate towards pessimism and despair.

One simple way to encounter negative situations is to repeat the *mantra*: This too, shall pass away. Allow your thoughts to turn to God, to dwell on His love and mercy. Such thoughts will help to elevate your mind and energize your spirits. Do not dwell on the negative situation, but allow the love of God to flood your mind, to cleanse it of all negativism, to fill you with hope and faith and peace.

Pessimism degrades you and defeats you. Optimism, born out of the understanding that God's divine plan is being worked out in your life, will, ultimately, lead you to liberation. You reach the glorious realization: *Tat Twam Asi*: That art Thou! Thou art the *Brahman*! Thou art the eternal, immortal Self!

This is the very pinnacle of optimism!

One of the vital requirements in the process of thought-control, is conquest over ego. When ego, the lower self – asserts itself, it drags the mind down with it. It restricts our consciousness and erects barriers on the path of our spiritual progress.

Raja yoga suggests four positive attitudes that will help us retain our sense of balance and equanimity. They are *maitri* (friendship towards our fellow human beings); *mudita* (joyous respect towards spiritual superiors); *karuna* (compassion towards those who are less evolved than we are); and *upeksha* (indifference towards those who are crude).

GOD IS WATCHING YOU!

One way to be vigilant in all that we think and say and do, is to be aware that God is omnipresent and omniscient, and is aware of all that we do. I am reminded of a little boy who was visiting his grandmother. There was a large picture of Sri Vishnu on the wall of her living room. Underneath the picture was the caption: *God is Watching You.*

The little boy became strangely quiet and subdued on seeing the picture. Noticing his mood, his grandmother asked him what the matter was.

"I suppose I must be good and behave myself here," replied the little boy. "If God is watching me, He is sure to punish me if I'm naughty."

"Not at all!" laughed the grandmother. "God is watching you all the time because he loves you so much that he can't take his eyes off you!"

This is the spirit with which we must cultivate good thoughts and positive emotions. Here is one of the simple prayers I often offer:

Tiny is the house of my heart,
O Lord, widen it that it may receive Thee!
Broken is the house of my heart – renew it,
That it may be worthy of Thee!
Unclean is the house of my heart:
May it be washed whiter than snow!
My deepest longing will be fulfilled
When Thou wilt dwell in the house
Of my heart forever and forever more – and I shall live and move
And do my daily work in Thy radiant presence, Lord!

AS YOU SOW ...

As you sow, so shall you reap. Therefore, be aware of every little thing that you do. Your desires, your thoughts, your fancies and your emotions are all seeds you are sowing in the field of life. Some of these seeds germinate instantly, and their effect is discernible at once. Some take a long time to grow, and we do not realize their effect for a long while. Consider, for example, a dinner-party to which you have been invited. Tempted by the tasty fare, you indulge yourself and overeat. Indigestion follows very soon, and you wake up at midnight, calling desperately for the doctor, sick and worried that you are dying of a heart-attack. Here, indigestion follows our eating immediately – action and reaction follow each other. We have reaped what we sowed a few hours earlier. But there are some actions of ours, whose effect we will feel only after several years – perhaps, after several births. Therefore, let us act with caution and wisdom.

Everyday, spend some time in silence, preferably at the same time and same place. Sitting in silence, go over all that you did in the past twenty-four hours. It is helpful if you go over your actions in the reverse order – i.e. think of what you did just a while ago, then of what you did a little earlier and so on. You will surely find that there were things which you did which you should not have done; as also things which you did not do but should have done – many errors of omission and commission. Repent for all your errors and pray to the Lord, "O Lord, give me the strength and wisdom not to repeat my errors." When this prayer is uttered from the depths of our being, God will surely bless our efforts.

TAKE CARE OF YOUR *SANGA*

If you wish to evolve spiritually, if you wish to sow good *karma*, take care of your *sanga* – the people with whom you associate. If your company is right and good, your actions will also be right and good. Bad company will lead you to evil; good company will lead you on the path of virtue. In the stormy ocean that is *sansar sagar* (the sea of earthly life), sage *Vashista* tells us, *satsang* is like a boat that can carry us safely across to the other shore. It not only keeps you afloat in safety, but also transports you across to the other shore.

The value of *satsang* cannot be underestimated. Therefore does sage *Vashista* describe *satsang* as the personification of one of the gatekeepers of the heaven world:

"If you wish to enter the palace (ie attain liberation)," the sage tells Sri Rama, "you must make friends with the gatekeeper."

Narada, the sage whose life was devoted to his Lord Narayana, was on one of his pilgrimages. One night, he received the hospitality of a poor, childless couple, who served him with deep love and piety. In the morning, when Narada was about to depart, the householder humbly begged him, "You are beloved of Lord Vishnu. O please tell Him to bless us with a child."

Narada was so moved by the request that he made a beeline to Vaikunth, where he met Lord Vishnu. "Dear Lord, be merciful to this humble devotee of yours. Bless that man with a child," implored the sage.

"I am sorry," said the Lord. "It is not in the destiny of that man to have a child."

Narada went on his way, disappointed.

Five years later, happening to pass the same way, he was once again received by the hospitable couple. To his amazement, he saw not one, but two children playing at the door of the hut.

"Whose children are these?" he asked in disbelief.

"Ours", said the man. "Soon after you left us last time, our prayers were answered. My wife and I have been truly blessed."

Narada hastened to confront Lord Vishnu. "How could you be so mistaken?" he shouted. "You said it was not in the destiny of that man to have children! Now he has two of them!"

The Lord laughed aloud. "That must be the doing of a saint," he said. "Surely you know Narada, association with a saint has the power to change destiny!"

Satsang can be translated to mean association with the good, the pure, the wise and the holy. Regular association with such positive, healing forces can lead us on to discrimination (*viveka*) and hence to liberation (*mukti*).

Satsang works effectively to promote our spiritual well being. As we begin to relish the good counsel and the good thoughts that we imbibe in the *satsang*, we become more and more aware of the truth of human life. When our minds are illumined by the light of truth, we become equipped to face what Shakespeare described as "the heartaches and thousand natural shocks that flesh is heir to" – in other words, all the miseries that confront us in human life. *Satsang* is like the lamp that lights our way through the darkness of our life on earth.

A realized soul, an enlightened one, is like a centre of Light – a living temple of the Lord towards which seekers travel, to find solace, comfort and good counsel. Since times immemorial, the devout of our land have sought out the abodes of the Lord, which have become centres of pilgrimage. The presence of a guru transforms the *satsang* into such a temple. Just as the temple is made holy by the living faith of the devout, so also is *satsang* made holy by the living presence of a *satguru*.

Indian culture and tradition have always emphasized the importance of the guru in the individual's search for liberation. This is because the intellect, on its own, cannot help us attain the truth. On the other hand, association with a saint will help us imbibe the truth we seek. From the presence of such a one, we assimilate goodness and virtue. When we have found such a noble soul, we need look no further.

Avidya (ignorance) and *kama* (desire) lead us on to bad *karma*. *Satsang* is the means by which we can conquer *avidya* and *kama*, thereby freeing our souls from the fetters of bad *karma*. All the negative aspects of our personality, like envy, greed, hatred and despair are driven out of our system when we enter the *satsang*. Distraction and temptation cease to trouble us. We are filled with the quality of *satva*.

Satsang is one of the most potent means of energizing and elevating your subconscious mind, through powerful spiritual vibrations that emanate from the guru. This is reinforced by the faith and devotion of one's fellow aspirants who congregate there. Such good association can only do us good, by aiding our moral and spiritual growth.

Our great spiritual teachers liken the pull of *maya* to the gravitational force of the earth. The *atman* must ultimately free itself from this force in order to attain liberation. *Satsang* provides us with the strong spiritual upliftment that we need for this purpose. Just as rocket scientists work hard to increase the velocity of a spacecraft, so also the people who come together at the *satsang* cultivate spiritual understanding and divine guidance, to help each other progress, and attain a higher plane.

We are constantly in touch with the lives and experiences of great souls and saintly personalities that are narrated in the *satsang*. This helps us realize that pain, suffering, defeat and adversity are not specific to our lives alone, and that virtue and goodness always triumph over negative forces.

Little wonder then, that Sant Tulsidas tells us that if you were to place all earthly and heavenly joys on one side of the scale, and the happiness of *satsang* on the other, the latter will outweigh the former. For human happiness is like cotton – bulky but insubstantial; while *satsang* is like a diamond – dense and strong, valuable and eternal.

ACCEPT! ACCEPT! ACCEPT!

Imbibe the spirit of acceptance. Accept all that happens to you as the Will of God. By accepting all that happens to us in the right spirit, we are settling the accounts of our previous *karma*, and making sure of good *karma* for our future. There are so many things in life that we cannot understand or come to terms with; the loss of a loved one, a sudden illness, or an unexpected accident. Instead of wasting our time and effort on the why and wherefore of such events, let us accept them in the spirit of surrender. For we must never ever forget this – that we are only reaping what we have sown. When we accept life's incidents and accidents in this spirit, our sorrows and sufferings are considerably mitigated. On the other hand, if we try to resist them or defy them, our misery only deepens.

Fighting pain and sufferings with egotistic rigidity serves no purpose. Ultimately, this kind of rigidity will break our hearts and minds.

There is a beautiful story told to us in the *Mahabharata*. It is said that the God of the Ocean once said to the River Ganga, "O Ganga! You bring with you huge banyan and oak trees as you flow into me. Why is it that you don't bring me some of those tender, delicate herbs that grow on your banks?"

The Ganga replied, "Those tender herbs you speak of may appear frail and weak, but, even though my water sweeps over them with force, they only bow down low before me, allowing me to flow past. Oaks and banyans, on the other hand, stand up against my flood, and I break them by their roots."

Egoistic defiance will only break you. On the other hand, humility and acceptance will give you the strength to resist adversity. If you bend, you cannot be broken!

Accept! Accept! Accept! When you cultivate the spirit of acceptance, you move towards the goal of *samata* or equanimity. *Samata* implies balance, serenity and tranquility, which are born out of spiritual understanding. And therefore, Sri Krishna declares in the Gita: *Samatvam yoga uchyate* – Equanimity is called Yoga.

When you lose your inner balance, you allow the world to overwhelm you, conquer you. When you retain your mental balance, you emerge the winner, even in the most trying of circumstances.

It is not adversity, but also prosperity that topples our sense of balance. When we meet with success repeatedly, we grow egoistic and arrogant. We tend to overlook God's grace and develop a false sense of superiority.

Adversity on the other hand, brings out the worst of our negative emotions – fear, despair, misery and insecurity. We lose all sense of objectivity, and succumb to self-pity.

Thus, when we lack equanimity or the spirit of acceptance, both prosperity and adversity lead only to misery and disillusionment. Let us instead, cultivate the spirit of humility in good times and bad times. Remember, every event, every incident has a reflection of God's mercy. It is His omnipotence that confers upon us both prosperity and adversity. Both are needed to help us unfold our spiritual strength. Both can prompt us towards good *karma*. When we accept all that happens to us as God's Will, we learn to live and act in the true spirit of a *karma yogi*.

Prosperity and adversity don't come to us by chance. They are the effect of our own *karmic* attainments. But both conditions can prove positive and helpful to our spiritual progress, if we turn to God in the spirit of acceptance and surrender. When we face adversity in the right frame of mind, we gain will power, patience, determination and detachment. All great achievers will testify that it was because of their adversities that they evolved towards greatness. Thus negative *karma* need not be a stumbling block for us!

Equally, prosperity is not something to be complacement about. We can make use of it to help others, serve suffering humanity, and learn to become selfless; we can utilize our leisure and good fortune to devote time to reflection and meditation. Saint Kabir emphasizes this when he says: "Everyone turns their mind to God in adversity, but not in prosperity. If one were to turn to God in prosperity, there would be no room for adversity!"

Acceptance of God's Will should not be passive and helpless – but joyous and positive. In fact, we should learn to praise God and thank Him for His infinite mercy, because He knows what is best for us. One of my favouvrite prayers is this:

> Thou knowest everything Beloved!
> Let Thy Will always be done!
> In joy and sorrow, my Beloved,
> Let Thy will always be done!

It has been said that the greatest saint in the world is not he who prays or fasts the most; nor even he who gives most alms; but he who is always thankful to God, who receives everything as an instance of God's goodness, and has a heart always ready to praise God for it.

William Law tells us, "If anyone would tell you the shortest, surest way to all happiness and perfection, he must tell you to make it a rule to thank and praise God for everything that happens to you. Whatever seeming calamity happens to you, if you thank and praise God for it, you turn it into a blessing. If you could work miracles, you could not do more for yourself, for with this thankful spirit, you will turn all that you touch into happiness!"

LEAVE IT TO GOD

There is a Chinese story of an old farmer, who had a weak, ailing horse for ploughing his field. One day, the old horse ran away to the hills.

The farmer's neighbours pursed their lips and offered their sympathy to him. "Such rotten luck!" they remarked.

"Bad luck? Good luck? Who knows?" replied the farmer, philosophically.

A week later, the old horse returned, bringing with it a herd of wild horses from the hills. This time, the neighbours swarmed around the farmer to congratulate him on his good luck.

"Good luck? Bad luck? Who can tell?" was his reply.

Sometime later, while trying to tame one of the wild horses, the farmer's only son fell off its back and broke his leg.

Everyone thought that this was bad luck indeed.

"Bad luck? Good luck? I don't know," said the farmer.

A few weeks later, the king's army marched into the village and conscripted every able-bodied young man living there. The farmer's son, who was laid up with a broken leg, was let off, for he would be of no use to them.

Now what could this be – good luck or bad luck? Who can tell?

Something that seems to be bad on the surface may actually be good in disguise. And something that seems to be attractive and 'lucky' may actually be harmful to our best interests. The wise ones leave it to God to decide what is best for them. They know that all things turn out good for them. They know that all things turn out good for those who love God and accept His Will unconditionally.

DO YOUR DUTY!

Do your duty. When you perform your duty consciously and with full responsibility, your inner instrument is purified.

Do your duty – but develop the spirit of detachment. Attend to your duty in the full awareness that nothing, no one, belongs to you. You are only an actor – and also a spectator – in the ever unfolding, cosmic drama of life. You must play this double role as actor and spectator

Once, a young woman complained to me, "My mother-in-law makes my life miserable. No matter how hard I try, I cannot please her. She treats me so badly that I am desperate. What shall I do?"

"You must treat her well," I said to her. "Show love and mercy to her."

"But she is wicked and cruel," the woman protested.

"She is acting as per her past *karma*," I replied. "I suggest that you sow the seeds of good *karma* by treating her well. Do your duty by her, irrespective of how she treats you. This way, you will ensure the security of your own future."

Do your duty. This is not the rule for the individual alone; it applies to all, to the whole society, to the nation, to the world at large. Kings and Emperors who failed to realize this, were reduced to naught – for they failed to do their regal, political duty as they ought to have done.

BE LIKE THE TIGER, NOT THE FOX!

A man was walking through a forest, and came across a fox which had lost its legs. He wondered how the animal could survive in such a state.

Soon thereafter, he saw a tiger coming to the same place with game in its mouth. The tiger ate its fill, leaving the rest for the fox.

The man observed the fox for a few days. Every day he saw that God sent the tiger to feed the fox. The man was struck with the wonder that was God's providence. He decided, "I too shall be like the fox. I shall lie in a corner, trusting the Lord to give me all I need!"

He did this for a month. And sure enough, he was close to death when a voice whispered in his ear: "You are on the path of error! Open your eyes to the truth! Be like the tiger, not the fox!"

Let us do our duty. God will do His! When Jesus urged his disciples to be like the lilies of the field, he did not mean that they should give up on their duty. He only urged them not to give in to constant worry and care.

We all know the wonderful proverb, "God helps those who help themselves." Let us therefore continue to do our duty; God will take care of the rest.

A pious man saw a naked child on a street, hungry and shivering in the cold. He become angry and said to God, "How can you allow such a thing to happen? Why can't you do something about this?'

God's answer came to him, loud and clear: "I certainly did something. I made you!"

John Ruskin said, "Every duty we omit, obscures some truth we should have known."

There is a legend of a monk, who once beheld the glorious vision of God in his lonely cell. As he was gazing with rapture at the vision, he heard the bell that summoned him to his daily duty – distributing loaves of bread to all the poor people in the village.

With agony, he tore himself away from the glorious vision to attend to the daily, dull routine of his duty. But when he came back, he was surprised and elated to find that God was still there, waiting for him to come back! God met him with the greeting, "I waited for you, because your duty called you. If you had not answered the call of duty, I would have departed!"

"What is the secret of your success?" someone asked George Washington Carver.

"I pray as if everything depends on God," he said. He paused and then added, "I work as if everything depends on me!"

Hence, we have the saying: Pull and pray!

ATTITUDE COUNTS!

A distinguished visitor arrived at a quarry where poor labourers were toiling hard. He went up to a few of them and asked just one question of each man: "What are you doing?"

The first one snarled angrily, "Can't you see I am breaking stones?"

The second one wiped the sweat off his brow and replied, "I am earning a living to feed my wife and children."

The third man looked up at him and said cheerfully, "I am helping to build a beautiful temple!"

You can imagine which one of the three men was creating good *karma* – although all of them were doing the same job!

George Macdonald said: "I find that doing my duty – doing the Will of God – leaves me no time for disputing His plans!"

Another name for doing God's Will is 'duty'. Duty simply means concentrating on what is God's Will for us now.

As Sri Krishna unfolds his doctrine of *karma* in the Gita, the very first thing he insists on is *devotion to one's duty*. "Do your duty, O Arjuna!" says the Lord. The name given in the Gita for duty is *swadharma*. "One's own *swadharma*, though imperfect, is better than the *dharma* of another, well discharged. Better death in one's *swadharma*; the *dharma* of another is full of fear."

(Chapter 3, Shloka 35)

And again, "Devoted each to his own duty, the man attains the highest perfection."

(Chapter 18, Shloka 45)

But the Lord lays down the most important condition when He insists on determination:

> Seek to perform your duty; but do not lay claim to its fruits. Be
> you not the producer of the fruits of *karma*...

Herein lies the secret of the turning point in our lives, from *preya* to *shreya*. In itself *karma* is not evil; it becomes evil when it is mixed up with desire. Verily, desire-tainted action leads continually to the wheel of birth and death. Even those who seek the heaven-world, says Sri Krishna, are slaves of desire. Therefore, we must not seek after the fruits of performing our *swadharma*. Freedom from desire is the ultimate freedom. He who does not desire the fruits of his *karma* is the conqueror of desire!

The sacred *Upanishads* sum up the essence of our duties to all:

> Let there be no neglect of Truth. Let there be no neglect of *dharma*.
> Let there be no neglect of welfare. Let there be no neglect of
> prosperity.
> Let there be no neglect of study and teaching.
> Let there be no neglect of the duties to the Gods and the ancestors.

Taittriya Upanishad

YAMAS AND NIYAMAS

Today, we often hear of senior executives in multinational firms being dismissed from their posts and replaced by others who are more amenable to the company's rules – the corporate code of conduct, as it is called. We go to banks and insurance firms, and we see that people who deal with us are normally polite and courteous. If they were not, they too would soon be replaced by others. As responsible employees, they follow a code of conduct while on duty.

Is there not a code of conduct for us if we wish to live a successful life in moral and spiritual terms? The Hindu scriptures give us such an ethical guideline, through *yamas* and *niyamas* (restrictions and observances). They are the essence of our duty to ourselves and others – the do's and dont's that are fundamental to a life of *dharma*.

Here are the *yamas* – the don'ts.

1. Practise *ahimsa* (non-injury). Do not harm others by thought, word or deed.
2. Practise *satya* (truth). Refrain from lying and breaking promises.
3. Practise *asteya* (non-stealing). Do not steal or covet what belongs to another.
4. Practise *brahmacharya* (celibacy). Do not be promiscuous in thought, word or deed.
5. Exercise *kshama* (patience). Do not be intolerant and insensitive to others.

6. Practise *dhriti* (steadfastness). Overcome inertia, indecision and changeability
7. Practise *daya* (compassion). Conquer cruelty and callousness towards all beings.
8. Practise *arjava* (honesty). Renounce all forms of deception and wrong doing.
9. Practise *mitahara* (moderation in appetite). Don't eat too much, don't consume food of violence.
10. Practise *saucha* (purity). Avoid impurity in mind, body and speech.

The ten practices recommended by the *niyamas* are the following.

1. *Hri* (remorse): Recognize your errors, confess and make amends. Apologise to those whom you have hurt. Accept correction.

2. *Santosha* (contentment): Nurture contentment, seeking happiness in what you are and what you have. Cultivate the attitude of gratitude.

3. *Dara* (giving): "Give, give, give!" was the *mantra* emphasised by my Beloved Master, Sadhu Vaswani. Give liberally and generously, without any thought of reward or recognition.

4. *Astikya* (faith): Cultivate firm, unshakable faith in God and your guru. Trust in the scriptures and in the wisdom of the saints.

5. *Ishvara–pujana* (worship): Cultivate devotion through daily prayer and meditation.

6. *Siddhanta–Shravana* (spiritual listening): Be eager to listen to the scriptures. Study their teachings. Choose a guru and obey his teachings implicitly.

7. *Mati* (cognition): Develop spiritual will and firm intellect under the guidance of your guru. Strive constantly for knowledge of God.

8. *Vrata* (sacred vows): Embrace religious observances and never waver in fulfilling them. Honour your vows as spiritual contracts with God.

9. *Japa* (recitation): Choose your sacred *mantra*, and chant it daily. Recite the sacred sound, word or phrase given to you by your guru.

10. *Tapas* (austerity): Practise discipline in your daily life. Practise self-denial, so that you may light the spark of transformation within you.

The *yamas* and *niyamas* have come down to us through the ages. They form the very foundation on which we should build our lives. They are fundamental to all living beings, who seek to attain life's highest aim – freedom from the bonds of *karma*, and attainment of the higher consciousness.

BE VIGILANT!

Live in awareness all the time. It was the Buddha who said to his disciples on one occasion, "Be aware! Be vigilant even when you are asleep. Watch your every thought and word and deed, and be aware of yourself!"

Evil thoughts and passions enter weak minds as easily as rain enters the house through a hole in the roof. This is the law of *karma* – for *karma* is even like a boomerang that inevitably returns to the sender.

More often than not, it is our thought, our intention that determines the kind of *karma* we create for ourselves. Therefore, we must learn to be aware of the motivation, the impulse that leads us to act or speak in a particular manner. Very often, we are unconscious of our intentions and this may create a bad *karmic* environment.

Consider, for example, the case of a man who is trying to give up smoking. Half way through the working day, he feels the urge to smoke. He borrows a cigarette from a friend, lights up and inhales deeply. Then suddenly, he remembers his decision to quit smoking. Without being aware of it, he has gone through all the habitual motions of lighting a cigarette. It is just not possible to change negative behaviour patterns, unless and until we are aware of everything we say, do and think.

Habits, especially bad habits, are hard to break. Take the H̲ away from habit, *a bit* remains. Take the *A* away, *bit* still remains; take *B* away, *it* will remain. Take *I* away, *T* will still remain! Many of us can't give up the habit of drinking Tea!

CULTIVATE CONSCIOUSNESS!

It is only when we are conscious and aware, that we can alert ourselves before an unconscious intention translates itself into action. As the saying goes, there is no use locking the stable after the horses have run away!

As we learn to be vigilant, we become aware of our own thoughts and intentions. We will begin to realize when, and in what situations, we fall prey to negative emotions like jealousy, envy, fear and anger. We will also understand when and why we are moved by positive emotions like compassion, love and generosity.

As we become conscious of our intentions – especially those that motivate us to action – we become better aware of the *karma* we are creating for ourselves. And when we are aware, when we are vigilant, the fruit of our actions becomes manifest to us. We become conscious of the law of cause and effect, and we clearly perceive that when our actions are motivated by hatred or jealously, they inevitably bring suffering upon us. On the other hand, when we are motivated by love, goodwill or compassion, our actions bring joy to us and others. Thus we realize that by paying attention to our thoughts and intentions as motivating forces, we are shaping our own daily lives.

Let me repeat to you, every day we are sowing the seeds of our *karma*. The only way to exercise any influence on our *karma* is by becoming alert and vigilant about our intentions. What we do with our hearts, can change our *karma*, it can change our life. Not only that, it can change the lives of everyone around us. All of us are interconnected. Our actions and reactions affect others; we can hurt or heal others by what we do.

YOU ARE WHAT YOU THINK

Two American soldiers had been prisoners of war in Japan during the II World War. Eventually they both survived, and went on to lead their lives back home. They met at a reunion 50 years later, in 1995. By now, Japan and US were actually allies. Everything had changed. One asked the other, "Have you forgiven those who imprisoned you?"

"No, I haven't," replied the second man vehemently. "Never, never shall I forgive them."

"In that case," said the first man softly, "somehow you are still in their prison."

The Buddha's teachings in the great *Dhammapada* begins with these memorable lines:

We are what we think.
All that we are arises with our thoughts.
With our thoughts we make the world.
Speak or act with an impure mind
And trouble will follow you
As the wheel follows the ox that draws the cart.
We are what we think.
All that we are arises with our thoughts.
With our thoughts we make the world.
Speak or act with a pure mind
And happiness will follow you
As your shadow, unshakable.

Being vigilant, being ever mindful of our actions also involves the sphere of our vocation – our professional life.

Thus, Buddhist thinker Thich Hanh warns us: "Do not live with a vocation that is harmful to humans and nature. Do not invest in companies that deprive others of their chance to live. Select a vocation that helps you realize the ideal of compassion."

RIGHT LIVELIHOOD

Truer words were never spoken. Unless we are alert and vigilant, we will find ourselves offending the Cardinal Rule of Right Livelihood. When we practise a profession that harms either human beings or nature, we are inflicting physical and moral harm on them and ourselves!

You may argue that we live in a world where jobs are difficult to find. If I refuse to work with harmful chemicals, pesticides, or in the manufacture of arms and ammunition, I may have to remain unemployed!

Alas! Many of us do not see this clearly enough. Many of us are too cowardly to speak out. Such issues should be discussed at a global level, and new jobs should be created that are humane and responsible for the welfare of society. For example, consider the irony of western nations manufacturing weapons to sell to poor Third World countries, while people in these countries are starving for lack of food!

Every year in Pune, we organize a Peace March in connection with my Beloved Master's Birthday, which is celebrated as International Meatless Day and Animal Rights Day. Every year, people ask me the same question: What has meat-eating to do with world peace?

My answer is always the same: "All killing is a denial of love. For to kill or to eat what another has killed, is to rejoice in cruelty. And cruelty hardens our heart and blinds our vision, and we see not, that they whom we kill are our brothers and sisters in the one brotherhood of life!"

Observing even one day in the year as Meatless day, helps many people to become vigilant and aware of the cruelties that are perpetrated on animals day after day. Indeed, I am happy to tell you that quite a few people who pledged to go Meatless for just one day, have subsequently abstained from all food of violence for a lifetime!

Vigilance helps us develop the ideal of compassion. We must try to stop all killing – however difficult such an ideal may be to achieve!

When we become vigilant, we realize too, that wars result from lack of reverence for life, lack of respect for others' rights. When we begin to observe the precept of no killing in our own daily life, we can work to bring out the larger issues of war and peace to the nation and to the world at large.

Prof. Peroux, a distinguished French Scholar, tells us that the amount of barley and rye used in western countries to make liquor, and feed cattle, is truly enormous. If meat and alcohol consumption in the West is reduced by 50%, he observes, the grain that becomes available would be enough to wipe out hunger and malnutrition in the Third World!

Studies also show, that if the world's nations stopped spending such huge sums of money on weapons, rockets, missiles and bombs, we would have more than enough money to eradicate many dangerous diseases, as well as evils like illiteracy.

But in the mechanical, mad rush of modern life, how many of us have the time to look deeply into such matters? How many of us take care to be vigilant about the principle of non-violence?

A teacher was once asked whether she would give up her job to become a butcher instead. The lady was deeply offended. "Don't you know that I belong to a noble profession?" she snapped. "How dare you ask me to take up such a degrading job?"

If the teacher had been more vigilant, she would have been aware of the concept of collective responsibility. If she and her children were meat-eaters, they would, in a very definite sense, share some responsibility for the butcher's "degrading" job of killing!

LIVE IN THE PRESENT

Today in the modern world, we all lead "extremely busy lives" as we love to tell everyone. "There's no time!" is the repeated refrain we hear all around us. Executives wish that the day had *28* hours; housewives wish that the children would stay in school longer; even children wish to stay up late and watch TV for some more time!

Oh yes, we are all extremely busy, even though we have all kinds of gadgets and electronic aids to do our work much faster. We don't do much manual work any more. But then, we don't seem to have any time for ourselves! Can I ask you how many of you meditate daily? Can I ask you how many of you sit in a silence corner and recite your favourite *shloka* or *mantra* daily? Can I ask you how many of you take time out to go for a walk?

I know quite a few people who tell me we don't have time to eat during the day. I do believe them! They go through endless cups of coffee and tea, skipping breakfast or lunch. May be, they "grab a sandwich" as they are working – but that's about all!

Why is this happening to us? Is there anything we can do about it? Can we possibly take control of our lives and slow down the pace so that we are aware of the present?

Let us cultivate greater awareness, so that we live in the present, and enjoy everything that we do – whether it is drinking tea, washing dishes, cooking, walking, talking or just sitting quietly.

True, human life is full of pain and suffering. But equally, it is also filled with many wonders and joys. Sunshine, laughter, music, the green grass, the company of our friends, the presence of our loved ones – the list is endless.

If we are not happy, if we are not at peace with ourselves, we cannot share peace and joy with those around us. It is only when we begin to radiate peace and joy, that we spread positive vibrations around us. This becomes possible when we cultivate awareness. This helps us to create good *karma*.

DO GOOD TO OTHERS

Do as much good as you can, to as many as you can, in as many ways as you can, as often as you can. People everywhere, bear the burden of misery and suffering. Lighten their loads, carry their burdens for them! Help as many as you can, to lift their load on the rough road of life. The day on which you have not helped a brother here, a sister there, is a lost day indeed.

Swami Vivekananda tells us that this earth is called *karma-bhumi* – the sphere of *karma*. If this be so, then it is up to us to choose bad or good *karma*. Thus, the world offers us the best chance to work out our own *karma*, and evolve towards perfection. This is why human life is regarded as the greatest gift – it offers us the opportunity to perfect ourselves.

All of us promote good *karma* in our day-to-day life, simply by performing acts of goodness, kindness, compassion and love. We must endeavour in every possible way to serve God in humanity – indeed, in all creation. All actions that are born out of good will, understanding, compassion and selflessness are good *karma*. When you perform such actions, they bring you peace and joy.

It has been said that when you share your joy with others, it doubles itself. When you share your knowledge and wisdom, you only become wiser. Therefore, give, give, give! Learn to share all that is good and worthwhile with others.

Seva-bhavna is the spirit of serving God in creation. This is done in an attitude of dedication and selflessness. It is no use to serve others with the expectation of reward or praise. Nor is it true service to help only those whom we love and consider to be our own people. He who is truly good, regards all creation as one family. He perceives God in all people, all creatures great and small. He regards all living creatures as his family members.

When you come to think of it, this too relates to the law of *karma*. For insight into *karma* will make us realize that in our numerous births and rebirths, we have had countless friends and relatives. How can we deny that we are *karmically* linked to hundreds, may be, thousands of people, across our various *janmas*? Why then, should we confine our loving, sharing and caring to a narrow circle of people whom we regard as our own?

Nor let us expect gratitude and praise from those whom we have served. Rather, it is we who must be thankful to them, for having given us the opportunity to do good *karma*, which is only to our own benefit! You may have spent your worldly wealth and physical effort in their service – but they have helped you gather spiritual wealth that is far more valuable, and boosted your effort to achieve liberation from the bonds of *karma*!

HELP YOUR BROTHER!

There is a moving story about Sadhu Sundar Singh, who was once travelling across the Himalayas with a companion. It was winter, and a severe blizzard was raging. The conditions were indeed very trying. As they trudged ahead, they saw a man lying still, by the narrow mountain path. To all appearances, he seemed to be frozen lifeless in the lonely terrain.

The Sadhu stopped to revive him and to offer whatever help he could. But his companion was adamant that they should move on. "It's no use wasting your time over him," he argued. "He is past reviving. If you stop to help him, you will be in trouble too, for it is suicidal to stop anywhere in this weather. We must push ahead so that we can reach the next village before it is dark."

But the Sadhu did not have the heart to leave the dying man to his fate. Resolutely, he began to rub and chafe the man's hands and feet, hoping to give some warmth to his cold limbs. His companion was so annoyed that he walked away from there, without even looking back.

Ten minutes of vigorous rubbing did nothing for the stranger. Finally, Sadhu Sundar Singh lifted the man on his back and began to trudge painfully through the falling snow.

Call it a miracle if you like – or call it good *karma* which fructifies instantly. The warmth of the exercise made the Sadhu's body temperature rise, and this gradually revived the stranger. The strain of carrying the man also helped the Sadhu to withstand the cold and the two mutually sustained each other.

When they had travelled a couple of miles, they saw another body lying by the wayside. It was the Sadhu's companion, who had refused to stop earlier. He was indeed frozen to death. Alone, he had not the warmth to fight the storm.

In Leo Tolstoy's story, "The Two Pilgrims", two Russians set out on a pilgrimage to the holy city of Jerusalem, determined to be present there during the solemn festivities of Easter. One of them was so intent on reaching there, that he stopped for nothing, and took thought of nothing but his destination. The other, as he passed through villages and towns, found many people who needed to be helped in one way or another, at every turn. He spent so much time, money and effort on the way, that he never really reached the Holy City. But the love of God had touched him, and through him, it touched the lives of all others with whom he came into contact. As for the other man, he participated in the Easter Celebrations at the Holy City – but he had failed to find God there!

MAKE YOUR LIFE BEAUTIFUL!

God has given us this rare and precious gift of human life that we may grow in perfection, awareness, and consciousness. Let us set aside our lower passions and desires and make an effort to progress on this path, for this is the true goal of life. Let us make the persistent effort to achieve this goal. This will give rise to *satvic* virtues in us. As we grow in *satvic* nature, our spirits will be cleansed and we will attain the state of the *stitha pragnya* that the Gita extols. This condition leads us on to *Brahma nirvana* where eternal joy and eternal peace can be ours. Each one of us has a birthright to attain this beautiful state.

According to Buddhist psychology our consciousness is divided into two parts – very much like a house built on two levels. On the ground floor is the 'living' room, which we may call 'mind-consciousness'. Below this is a basement, which we can call 'store-consciousness'. Here in this store, all that we have ever said, done, thought, felt and experienced is stored as in an archive. It is as if we sit upstairs in the living room, retrieve from below one film after another from the archive, and watch them!

Horror films like *Anger*, *Fear*, *Despair*, come up for viewing on their own. They seem to 'pop up' before us whether we want to see them or not. We are forced to spend much of our time watching these films – and they affect our mind-consciousness, our 'living space'. Indeed, I would go so far as to say that they are destroying our lives!

The Gita describes human life as *kshetra*, an area, a field, where every kind of seed can be planted – seeds of suffering, happiness, anger, pride, joy, peace or sorrow. The store consciousness is also filled with these same seeds. When a seed manifests itself in our minds, we can assume that it returns to the store, stronger than before. We can also assume, that it will return to haunt us again and again. The quality of our life, depends thus on the quality of the seeds we have in store.

Ask yourself – what are the seeds sprouting in your mind? Seeds of anger, sorrow or fear? Or seeds of joy, happiness and peace? We must cultivate wholesome seeds consciously. We have to water them, nourish them, and help them grow stronger.

Let me put it another way. Picture yourself standing near your window on a beautiful moonlit night. You look out at the night sky, you are filled with joy and peace and a sense of beauty. You stand there for five minutes, just enjoying the beautiful scene... during those five minutes, you have watered and nourished the seeds of peace, joy and beauty. During those five minutes, seeds of anger, sorrow and despair will not have been watered.

Friends, we must cultivate many such moments in our daily life. These seeds of joy and peace that manifest in our mind, grow stronger when they return to the store. These are wholesome, nutritious seeds, which we must water and cultivate consciously, so that our lives may be filled with peace and healing!

The trouble with many of us is that we constantly focus our attention on what is wrong with our lives. This is like constantly scratching and re-opening a fresh wound. How will the wound heal if we are constantly prodding and poking at it?

Let us then, live the life Beautiful! Let us create our own good *karma*! Let us consciously choose the *good* way, the *God-way*!

KARMA – FAQS

Q: Sadhu Vaswani has said that the principle of *karma* is that of a boomerang. Could you please explain?

A: There is an inviolable law which governs the universe from end to end. What you send, comes back to you! Do you gossip about another? You will be gossiped about! Do you send out thoughts of hatred and enmity to another? Hatred and enmity will come back to you, turning your life into a veritable hell! Do you send out loving thoughts to others? Do you pray for struggling souls? Do you serve those that are in need? Are you kind to passers-by, the pilgrims on the way, who seek your hospitality? Then remember, sure as the sun rises in the east, all these things will return to you, making your life beautiful and bright as a rose garden in the season of spring!

A boy who did not know what an echo was, cried across a valley: "Who is there?" The echo answered, "Who is there?"

The child could not see who spoke those words.

He asked, "Who are you?" Back came the words, "Who are you?"

The boy thought someone was trying to tease him. So he shouted, "Won't you stop it?" Back came his own words, "Won't you stop it?"

Exasperated, the child yelled an insult which was flung back into his face.

Just then, his mother explained to him that no one was trying to tease him, but that it was only the echo of his own voice which came back to him.

The child cried out, "I love you!" Back came the words, "I love you!"

The child shouted, "You are so good!" Immediately, the compliment was returned to him. And the child became happy.

What we give to this world comes back to us. Therefore, let us give love, kindness, help, sympathy and service and they will return to us, and we will stand strong as a towering lighthouse amidst the stormy waves of this world.

Q: How does bad *karma* originate?

A: Man was given free will, he was given the right of choice. He can choose between what the Upanishads call *preya* and *shreya*. *Preya* is the pleasant: the path of *preya* is the path of pleasure that lures us but leads us to our degradation. As a Danish proverb has it, "After pleasant scratching comes unpleasant smarting."

Shreya is the good: the path of *shreya* may, at first, be difficult to tread; but ultimately it leads to our betterment, well-being and spiritual unfolding. At every step man is given this choice. Many of us, alas, choose the easy path – the path of pleasure – and so we keep on multiplying undesirable *karma*.

Q: Can our bad *karma* be mitigated or lessened? Is there any hope for us?

A: Evil *karma* can be mitigated or lessened by *Nama-japa* and selfless service to those that suffer and are in pain, and above all, through the grace of God or a God-man.

Q: In the law of evolution, can a human being be re-born
    as an animal?

A: When the law of *karma* finds that a person is so
incorrigible that he will not be reformed until he goes back
to the stage of the animal, and begins again – it is only in
such cases that a human being is reborn as an animal.

I sometimes think about a classmate of mine. When I
was in the first standard, he was in the fourth. I came to the
second, he was still in the fourth standard. I went to the
third and he continued to be in the fourth. I went to the
fourth and he was my classmate. I went to the fifth and the
teacher said, "We must do something. This boy has been in
the fourth standard for so many years, let us send him back
to the third, so that he can gather some momentum."

I do not feel that anyone of you could have had that
experience. But it does happen in very few cases, where
people commit mortal crimes, for example killing little
children. Then perhaps, the law of *karma* gives us the body
of an animal so that we can restart the process. But it is
always for our own good.

Q: Why are our past *karmas* kept a secret from us?

A: Don't you think it is a great mercy of God that our
karmic links are not known to us? Else, it may be difficult
for us to live in this world. Thus, for instance, there may be
a man whose wife was his bitter enemy in an earlier
incarnation and has now become his wife only to settle
previous accounts. If all this were revealed to us, what would
be our condition?

Q: If all that happens today is the result of our past *karma*,
    does it mean that everything is predestined?

A: No, certainly not! We are the architects of our own
destiny, the builders of our own future. Many of us blame

fate, or *kismet* for our misfortunes. But let me tell you, that you are the builders of your own fate. Therefore, be careful, especially, of your thoughts. We pay scant attention to our thoughts, believing them to be of no consequence. We say, after all, it was only a thought, what does it matter? Every thought is a seed you are sowing in the field of life. What you sow today, you will have to reap in the near or remote future.

God has created a universe of beauty, fullness, happiness and harmony. Each one of us is a child of God. God wishes each one of us to be happy, prosperous, successful and to enjoy all the good things He has created. We keep ourselves away from all these bounties because of our *karma*. Change your *karma* and you will change the condition in which you live. And you can change your *karma* by adopting a new pattern of thinking.

Q: Can *karmas* be wiped off by *japa*?

A: It is believed that the effects of *karma* can be mitigated through *nama japa*. In any case, the suffering can be reduced, because *nama japa* acts as a sort of chloroform. It is like going through an operation. The surgeon puts you under anaesthesia and you come out of the operation without feeling the acute pain. Else the pain is so excruciating, that a person could die of it. This is what *nama japa* does to you.

Q: Can saints take over the *karma* of their disciples?

A: They can. However, normally, they do not wish to interfere with the law of *karma*. For they know that the law of *karma* does not wish to punish us for what we may have done in the past. The law of *karma* wishes to reform us and so sends us experiences which may help in our spiritual advancement. It is true there have been cases when men of God have taken the *karma*s of their devotees upon themselves. It is like buying birds and setting them free. Likewise, a man who is rich in the wealth of the Spirit may, if he so desires, pay for our *karma* and release us from the cage of *maya*.

Q: Does man get *mukti* (liberation from the cycle of birth and death) after working out his *karma*?
A: *Karma* leads to *karma*, the process of sowing and reaping goes on endlessly. But *mukti*, liberation, comes through the grace of God. Thus we have cases of sinners being suddenly transformed into saints. It was a Christian saint who said, "What God is by nature, man becomes by grace." Through grace, man becomes God-like, emancipated, free!

Q: Is there no shortcut to the ending of *karma*?
A: Yes. There are three ways. The first is the way of self-inquiry, to understand who you are. You are not the body, nor the mind. You are not the *buddhi*. You are *that* which cannot be touched by *karma*. Once you arrive at that stage all *karma* drops out.
    The other is the way of self-surrender.
    The third is the way of selfless service.
    Those are the three ways by which the store of *karma* can be burnt. But even then, the *prarabdha karma* (fructified *karma*) that you have brought with you into this life, has to be worked out. But the *sanchita karma*, the storehouse of *karma,* gets burnt.

Q: Don't you think it is very difficult for young people to accept these three points?

A: Then we have to keep entering the cycle of birth and death, until it becomes easy for us to do it. Experience teaches us. We have to pass through those experiences. Very few learn through vicarious experiences.

A parent says to the child, "My child, never do this. I did this and I repented." The child will not understand. He would like to do that and, from his own experience, learn what it is to repent after doing a particular thing. But there are some who learn from vicarious experience.

This whole life is a jail. We are prisoners. We think we are free but we are in bondage. We need to be liberated. To get *mukti*, you need *mumukshatva*, the desire, the intense longing, for liberation. That is very necessary. Until that arises, you don't want to be liberated. You are happy and satisfied with whatever life gives you.

There was a man. They asked him, "Why don't you desire to go to heaven?" He said, "Life must be boring there. Here it is exciting."

Q: If everything that happens to us is ordained by God, then how are we responsible for our actions?

A: So long as man has the egoistic feeling in his mind that he is the doer, he is responsible for his own actions. When he frees himself from the ego, transcends this feeling of doing, he becomes an instrument of God and all the responsibility for his actions belong to God.

Q: How do we know in any situation that it is God's Will taking effect and not our will?

A: There are certain things that happen to us. We do not want them to happen and try to avoid or escape them. But in spite of all our efforts, things happen. Those are the things that we should accept as God's Will. It is something that I did not want to happen. Yet it has happened. But there are other things that I do. For instance, I get angry with someone, I gossip, I spread wrong reports about a friend. That is my will. I am doing it.

Q: Tell us how to face suffering?

A: If our attention is on suffering, it gets magnified beyond all proportions. In the midst of suffering let us count our blessings. Usually, we suffer only in one area of our life. There are so many other things for which we should be grateful. Take a piece of paper and make a list of all the blessings you still have. There was a man who started from scratch and built up a flourishing business and one day became bankrupt. The first thing he did was to take up a piece of paper and write down all the things he still possessed. He found, he still had a great deal to be thankful for. With gratitude in his heart, he started anew and built up a still larger business. If we count our blessings, our suffering recedes in the background.

In all conditions of life, let us thank the Lord. Let us make it a habit – to praise the Lord at every step, in every round of life. Even in the midst of fear and frustrations, worry and anxiety, depression and disappointment, let these words come out of the very depths of our hearts: "Thank you, God! Thank you, God!" and we will be filled with a peace that will amaze us. When we thank the Lord all the time, we build for ourselves a ladder of consciousness on which we can climb and touch the very pinnacle of peace.

Let me tell you the story of a woman. Her husband fell seriously ill. The doctor despaired of his condition and said he would not be able to last longer than six months. The woman had deep faith in God and started thanking the Lord a thousand times everyday. "Thank you, God! Thank you,

God!" she prayed again and again. "Thank you, God, for having healed my husband and made him whole." She continued to offer this prayer even though there was no sign of healing in sight. Strange enough, a few months later, when the husband went for a check up, the doctors were amazed at his miraculous recovery. "A power above and beyond ours, has been at work!" they exclaimed.

Whatever be the condition in which you find yourself, whatever be the suffering through which you pass, keep on thanking the Lord all the time. When you do so, your heart expands and you become receptive to the helpful and healing forces of God.

In every situation, do the very best you can and leave the result to the Lord. When Henry Ford was seventy-five years old, he was asked the secret of his success. He answered: "My life is built in these three rules. I do not eat too much, I do not worry too much and, if I do my best, I believe that what happens, happens for the best."

KARMA IN THE NEW AGE

I received an anonymous letter written by someone who was present at one of my discourses on *karma*. In the course of the letter he writes: "Your talk outlines no new approach to the problem: Why do good people suffer? Many intellectuals present were rather disappointed. You asked us to repeat with you the words, "Thank you, God!" which, too was very frustrating. Is India entering the 21st century, or still looking back? When will blind faith be wiped off from the country?"

I confess I am not a scholar. I am not qualified to give intellectual interpretations. I do aspire to give *life-interpretations*. The law of *karma* is an eternal law: it is a universal law. It needs to be interpreted in life. Therefore, as I said, I am interested in a *life-interpretation* of this and other eternal laws.

I recall having read many years ago, concerning an eminent Confucian scholar. He was 80 years of age, and it was believed that no one could equal him in China in learning and understanding. One day he learnt that far, far away a new doctrine had sprung up that was profoundly deeper than his knowledge. This upset him. He lost his interest in life. He decided that the issue must be decided one way or the other. He undertook a long journey, traversed many miles and met the master of the new Zen school. He asked him to explain the new doctrine. In answer, the Buddhist monk said to him: "Venerated Sir, the doctrine we propagate is a very simple one. It can be summed up in one sentence: "To avoid doing evil, to do as much good as possible, this is the teaching of all the Buddhas'."

On hearing this, the old Confucian scholar flared up and said: "What do you mean? I have come here facing the dangers and hazards of a long, perilous journey and in spite of my advanced age. And you just quote a little jingle that every three-year-old child knows by heart! Are you mocking at me?" The Zen master very politely answered: "I am not mocking at you. But please consider that though every three-year-old child knows these words by heart, yet even a man of eighty fails to live up to them!"

It is life that is needed, not doctrines, creeds or dogmas. Do we bear witness to the great teachings in deeds of daily living? I recall an incident in the life of the eldest of the Pandava brothers. As boys, they went to an *ashrama* and the very first teaching passed on to them by their guru was: "*Satyam vad Krodham maakuroo!*" which means, "Speak the truth and never get angry!"

The next day the teacher asked the Pandava brothers if they had learnt the lesson. All of them except Yudhishtira, the eldest, said they had remembered the lesson. Yudhishtira, however, had not learnt the lesson. "The first half, I remember," he said diffidently. "But the latter half I have not yet been able to learn!" So, the teacher very patiently made him repeat the words, "*Krodham maakuroo! Krodham maakuroo!*"

But again, on the following day, when the teacher asked his students if they had remembered the teaching, Yudhishtira said he had not been able to memorise the second half of the lesson. Once again the Guru made him repeat the words: "*Krodham maakuroo! Krodham maakuroo!*"

This went on for a week. On the eighth day, when Yudhishtira insisted that he had not yet learnt the latter part of the teaching, the Guru lost his temper and shouted at him: "How can you be so stupid? Your younger brothers learnt the lesson on the very first day. Why is it that you cannot remember two simple words, *Krodham maakuroo?*"

Then it was that Yudhishtira clapped his hands in joy and said: "Sir, I can say now that I have learnt the lesson!" "How is it that a moment ago, you could not recall the words, and now you assert that you have learnt them?" asked the Guru, greatly surprised.

Yudhishtira said: "The first half of the lesson was easy to remember, because I always speak the truth. The latter half, viz, never yield to anger, I could not be sure if I had mastered, unless someone got angry with me, and in return, I remained calm. Today, I found that in the face of anger I was unruffled and so I can truthfully say that I have remembered the teaching."

Yes, it is life that is needed, not book learning, nor intellectual or psychological interpretations. Our friend writes in his beautiful letter that there is exploitation everywhere: exploitation and social injustice and suffering are due to the fact that we have not learnt to interpret the law of *karma* in our daily life. If we truly believed in the law of *karma*, there would be no exploitation, for the law of *karma* boldly declares: "He that exploits shall be exploited." If India is to be made new, what is needed is not new interpretations but translation of the teachings in our daily lives.

Only a few days ago, I visited a sick woman. She is not learned in the lore of books. She had a severe backache, excruciating pain at the base of the spine. She could neither sit nor stand, neither bend nor walk. Despite it all, there was a smile on her face as she said to me: "I must have done something during one of my earlier births to deserve this condition. Perhaps, I have beaten someone on the back with a stick. God save me from doing any evil in this birth."

This is the prayer of everyone who believes in the law of *karma*: "God save me from doing any evil!" And if this becomes the prayer of every man and woman in India, this ancient, unhappy land will become new and India will shine, once again, in the splendour of the new morning sun.

The root of exploitation, social injustice and maladministration is in the thought: I will get away with it! Once I know that in this open universe I cannot get away with anything, I shall be careful to see that there is no evil in my thoughts and actions.

I do an evil deed in the dark of the night, I say to myself: "No one saw it: I shall get away with it!" The law of *karma* tells me: It is true, no one saw it. But the seed has entered the field of my life. The field of my life has registered it. And one day or the other – today, tomorrow or in the distant future – out of the seed will grow a tree whose fruit will have to be eaten by me! Therefore, beware! Take care! Live and move and do your daily work in the ever-living presence of God!

This was the teaching that was given to every student in ancient India. There is an oft-repeated story of a guru and two disciples who came to him seeking admission to the *ashrama*. The guru gives them a coconut each and instructs them to break the coconut where no one may see them, and return with the broken pieces. One of the students enters a dark and solitary cave and, finding no one watching, breaks the coconut and within no time, returns to the *ashram*. The second disciple returns only after sunset and that, too, with the coconut intact. His friend says to him: "Why did you not accompany me? There were so many caves. I entered one of them. You could have entered another and broken the coconut. Nobody would have seen you." At this, the other friend replies: "I entered cave after cave, but wherever

I went, just as I was about to break the coconut, I found that
He was watching me. God was watching me! There was not
a nook or a corner where God was not!"

How many of us live in this consciousness? This is an
ancient interpretation of an ancient, eternal law. But how
many live up to it?

The students of the St. Mira's Primary School recite a
beautiful song in their sanctuary almost everyday:

Be careful little eyes what you see:
There's a Father up above,
Watching you in love,
So be careful little eyes what you see!
Be careful little ears what you hear:
There's a Father up above,
Watching you in love,
So be careful little ears what you hear!
Be careful little tongue what you speak:
There's a Father up above,
Watching you in love,
So be careful little tongue what you speak!
Be careful little hands what you do:
There's a Father up above,
Watching you in love,
So be careful little hands what you do!
Be careful little feet where you go:
There's a Father up above,
Watching you in love,
So be careful little feet where you go!
Be careful little mind what you think:
There's a Father up above,
Watching you in love,
So be careful little mind what you think!
Be careful little heart what you feel:
There's a Father up above,
Watching you in love,
So be careful little heart what you feel!

If only we lived in the thought that God is watching us, exploitation, social injustice and maladministration would be completely eradicated from the country.

Let me relate to you an incident from the life of a judge. He was an honest and God-fearing man. One day, he was offered a bribe of two hundred thousand rupees. It was a large amount and he succumbed to the temptation. However, his conscience kept pricking him all the time. It kept saying to him: "You have sold your soul for a mere two hundred thousand rupees!" Finally, unable to quieten his conscience, he went to the rich man's house and returned the entire amount to him, saying: "There's a Father up above, watching us with love, so our hands must not give or receive a bribe!"

How many of us would do likewise?

THUS SPOKE THE GREAT ONES

Deeds determine one's place in society. One becomes an outcast or a highly placed person by his deeds. Evil deeds are easy to do; good deeds are difficult; but the good deeds pay the highest rewards.

Buddhism

Man is known by his deeds, and is judged even so by God. God will reward good deeds and punish evil ones. To profess goodness is of no value; one must do good deeds or be condemned.

Christianity

Reward will follow every good deed. Only by doing good deeds can a man know the true joy of living and have a long life.

Confucianism

One becomes what one does. The doer of good deeds will become good and the doer of evil deeds will become evil. Action, the doing of the good, is superior to renunciation. Thus, at all times one should be doing good.

Hinduism

On the Day of Judgement every soul shall be judged in accordance with his deeds. To do good drives out evil.

Islam

The good show the way to others by their good acts. Each day passes never to return. Therefore, do good at all times, for you can never call back a day to perform a good deed that was not done.

Jainism

Do good at all times, for man will be judged by his works.

Judaism

Man's deeds are recorded by the divine. He becomes good in the eyes of the divine by doing good deeds. God is the source of good deeds.

Sikhism

As you sow, so shall you reap. This body is the result of your actions.

Sikhism

We come to the Wise One through good deeds. It is important that we keep ourselves physically fit to do good deeds at all times.

Zoroastrianism

Do not do unto others all that which is not well for yourself.

Zoroastrianism

Experiences of pleasure and of pain are the results of merit and demerit, respectively.

Patanjali

Every act must have its consequences. If anything comes your way by reason of *prarabdha*, you can't help it. If you take what comes, without any special attachment, and without any desire for more of it or for a repetition of it, it will not harm you by leading to further births. On the other hand, if you enjoy it with great attachment and naturally desire for more of it, it is bound to lead to more and more births.

Ramana Maharshi

A man's latent tendencies have been created by his past thoughts and actions. These tendencies will bear fruits, both in this life and in lives to come.

Patanjali

So long as the cause exists, it will bear fruits – such as rebirth, a long or short life, and the experiences of pleasure and of pain.

Patanjali

Every action that you do produces a two-fold effect. It produces an impression in your mind and when you die you carry the *Samskara* in the *Karmashaya* or receptacle of works in your subconscious mind. It produces an impression on the world or *Akashic* records.

Swami Sivananda

Men are not punished for their sins, but by them.

Elbert Hubbard

Whoso diggeth a pit shall fall therein.

Proverbs

The jealous are troublesome to others, but torment to themselves.

William Penn

Do good with what thou hast, or it will do thee no good.

William Penn

Watch your thoughts, for they become words.
Watch your words, for they become actions.
Watch your actions, for they become habits.
Watch your habits, for they become character.
Watch your character, for it becomes your destiny.

Anonymous

Those who are free of resentful thoughts surely find peace.

Buddha

Our life is what our thoughts make it.

Marcus Aurelius

People pay for what they do, and still more, for what they have allowed themselves to become. And they pay for it simply: by the lives they lead.

Edith Wharton

Luck is a word devoid of sense. Nothing can exist without a cause.

Voltaire

Any man will usually get from other men just what he is expecting of them. If he is looking for friendship he will likely receive it. If his attitude is that of indifference, it will beget indifference. And if a man is looking for a fight, he will in all likelihood be accommodated in that.

John Richelsen